Wicked
PHILADELPHIA

Wicked
PHILADELPHIA
SIN IN THE CITY OF BROTHERLY LOVE

THOMAS H. KEELS

Charleston | London

THE
History
PRESS

Published by The History Press
Charleston, SC 29403
www.historypress.net

Images are from the author's collection unless otherwise noted.

First published 2010
Second printing 2010
Third printing 2011

Manufactured in the United States

ISBN 978.1.59629.787.6

Keels, Thomas H.
Wicked Philadelphia : sin in the city of brotherly love / Thomas H. Keels.
p. cm.
Includes bibliographical references.
ISBN 978-1-59629-787-6
1. Philadelphia (Pa.)--History--Anecdotes. 2. Crime--Pennsylvania--Philadelphia--
Anecdotes. 3. Scandals--Pennsylvania--Philadelphia--Anecdotes. 4. Philadelphia (Pa.)-
-Biography--Anecdotes. I. Title.
F158.36.K44 2009
974.8'11--dc22
2009050438

CONTENTS

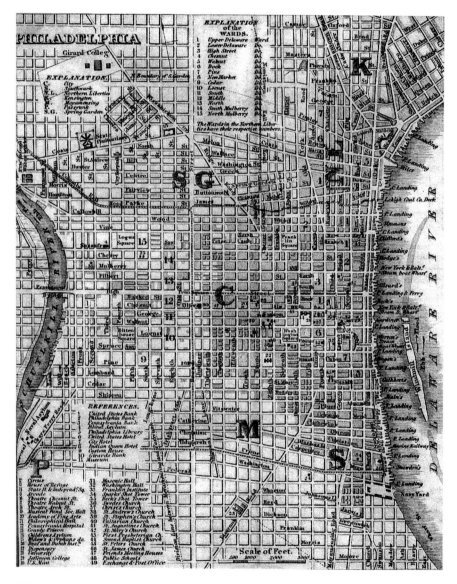

Philadelphia and environs, circa 1840. The city is indicated with a "C." Below it are Southwark ("S") and Moyamensing ("M"); above it are Kensington ("K"), Northern Liberties ("NL") and Spring Garden ("SG").

A NOTE ON GEOGRAPHY

Between 1682 and 1854, the city of Philadelphia consisted of a twelve-hundred-acre rectangle bordered by the Delaware River on the east, Vine Street on the north, the Schuylkill River on the west and Cedar (today South) Street on the south. The rectangle was divided into four quadrants by two major boulevards: Broad Street, running north and south, and High (later Market) Street, running east and west. These two avenues intersected at Centre Square, later known as Penn Square. Since 1871, Penn Square has been the location of City Hall.

The city's major east–west streets were named after native plants, although several were later renamed. From north to south, they were: Vine, Sassafras (today Race), Cherry, Mulberry (today Arch), Filbert, High (Market), Chestnut, Walnut, Locust, Spruce, Pine, Lombard and Cedar (South).

The north–south streets were numbered, except for the oldest ones along each river (Water and Front Streets on the Delaware, Ashton and Beach on the Schuylkill). Originally, streets east of Broad ran from Delaware Second to Delaware Thirteenth as you moved west. Streets west of Broad ran from Schuylkill First to Schuylkill Eighth as you moved east. In 1853, the City Councils finally realized how confusing this was and renumbered the streets consecutively from Second Street near the Delaware to Twenty-fourth Street near the Schuylkill. Just to keep things a little confusing, Broad Street continued to take the place of Fourteenth Street.

The fast-growing city was soon ringed by other boomtowns. Below South Street, rough-and-tumble Southwark ran along the Delaware, while

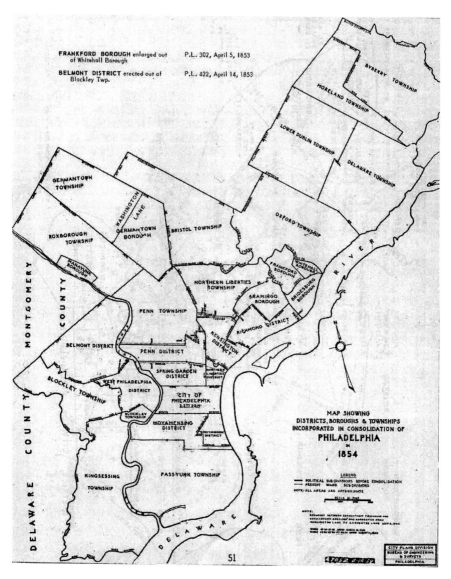

The patchwork of boroughs, townships and districts that constituted Philadelphia County prior to its consolidation with the city of Philadelphia in 1854.

semirural Moyamensing sprawled to the west. Above Vine Street, Northern Liberties stood to the east and Spring Garden to the west. In 1800, when Philadelphia was the largest city in the United States, Northern Liberties was the sixth largest and Southwark the seventh largest.

The rest of Philadelphia County was a patchwork of villages, districts, boroughs and townships, many predating the city itself. Passyunk Township occupied the southern tip of the city. Across the Schuylkill, West Philadelphia was ringed by Belmont District, Blockley Township and Kingsessing Township.

The Wissahickon Creek ran through the northwestern arm of the county, dividing rural Roxborough and the mill town of Manayunk in the south from the venerable settlement of Germantown to the north. During the nineteenth century, Germantown's northwestern end became known as Mount Airy and Chestnut Hill, home to the estates of the wealthy.

Along the Delaware River north of the city stood the ancient neighborhoods of Kensington, Richmond and Bridesburg, with Frankford and Oxford farther inland. The far northeast—which remained mostly rural until after World War II—consisted of Delaware, Lower Dublin, Moreland and Byberry Townships.

In 1854, the Act of Consolidation merged the city of Philadelphia with the surrounding county, creating its current boundaries and making it the largest American metropolis in terms of physical size at the time.

ACKNOWLEDGEMENTS

Like *Macbeth*, *Wicked Philadelphia* was born with the help of three midwives with a taste for the macabre: Diana Cammarota, the original editor and publisher of the *Rittenhouse Sq. Revue*; Dan Herman, her successor at the *Revue*; and Jim Cotter, host and producer of *Creatively Speaking*, the weekly arts and culture program on Temple University's WRTI-FM.

Most of the chapters in *Wicked Philadelphia* originated as articles in the *Revue* or radio features on *Creatively Speaking*. I owe Diana, Dan and Jim my deepest thanks for handing me a shovel and encouraging me to dig deep into the dark crevasses of my adopted city. This book would not have been possible without their support, creativity and friendship.

Hannah Cassilly of The History Press suggested the theme of *Wicked Philadelphia* and has worked with me closely to develop and shape this book. I am deeply grateful for her assistance.

I must also thank the following people for their help: Michael Angelo, archivist at Thomas Jefferson University; Adam Bell of the *Charlotte Observer*; Michael Brooks; Emily Cooperman; Brenda Galloway-Wright and the staff of the Urban Archives at Temple University; Mary Lou Hughes and the staff of the Free Library of Springfield Township (Montgomery County); Cornelia S. King, chief of reference at the Library Company of Philadelphia; Nancy R. Miller of the University of Pennsylvania Archives; James Mundy, archivist of the Union League of Philadelphia; David Rowland and Betty Smith of the Old York Road Historical Society; John Schimpf; Phillip Seitz, curator of History and Fermentation at Cliveden of the National Trust;

Acknowledgements

Brian Shovers, library manager of the Montana Research Center; Robert Morris Skaler; Nancy V. Webster; and Marie Brown Wilson of the Explore PA History Project.

As always, my deepest thanks go to my partner and friend, Lawrence M. Arrigale, for his help as photographer, editor and tech support; his unflagging enthusiasm and encouragement; and his infinite kindness, patience and love. Without him, I might easily have ended up as a chapter in this book!

INTRODUCTION

O that thou mayest be kept from the evil that would overwhelm thee, that faithful to the God of thy mercies in the life of righteousness, thou mayest be preserved to the end.
—*William Penn's Prayer for Philadelphia, 1684*

As this place hath growne more popular and the people more increased, Looseness and Vice Hath also Creept in.
—*Governor William Markham, 1697*

Philadelphia, more than other American cities, has always struggled with its split personality. There's altruistic Dr. Jekyll in his plain Quaker garb, founding almshouses, hospitals and libraries at the drop of a hat and then helping inner-city schoolchildren paint a mural. But around the corner is his brother, flashy Mr. Hyde, lusting after money, power, sex and every other worldly pleasure. He's the one charging the mural kids a rental fee for paints and brushes and inviting the older girls for a ride in his Hummer, the one with the blue municipal plates.

This duality dates back to November 1682, when William Penn, that weird combination of religious visionary and real estate entrepreneur, first set foot on American soil. He had come to claim Pennsylvania, his land grant from Charles II, and to establish its capital of Philadelphia, City of Brotherly Love. Penn's goals were twofold: to establish a New Jerusalem of peace and tolerance and to make a fortune through land sales. While the latter goal remained elusive, Penn nearly achieved the first.

One of Penn's first actions was to conclude treaties of friendship with the Lenni-Lenapes, the local Native Americans. These pacts set a standard for fairness and tolerance that has never been equaled in our country's history. They were the first step in the creation of a visionary "Holy Experiment" that would offer its participants guarantees of freedom unknown throughout the world. Not surprisingly, Philadelphia flourished. Nearly a century before Thomas Jefferson wrote of "Life, Liberty, and the pursuit of Happiness," Penn intuited that widespread prosperity walked hand in hand with personal security, freedom of conscience and respect for others.

It was too good to last. Penn died in England in 1718, penniless and sick. When his sons became Proprietors of Pennsylvania, the Holy Experiment died. With the assistance of James Logan and other officials, the younger Penns conspired to cheat the Lenni-Lenapes out of more than 700,000 acres in northeastern Pennsylvania. They had already begun to sell this land to cover their debts, so they had to get clear title to it somehow. They did so with a combination of tailored treaties, well-paid witnesses and professional athletes who turned the traditional Indian method of demarcating land purchases with a casual stroll into a thirty-six-hour marathon that covered fifty-five miles.

At the end of the Walking Purchase of September 1737, the Penns had grabbed twelve hundred square miles of prime Lenni-Lenape hunting lands along the upper Delaware and Lehigh Rivers. They had also poisoned relations with their former allies (now branded as weaklings in the eyes of enemy tribes) and triggered ongoing warfare between natives and settlers in once-peaceful Pennsylvania. And they had obliterated their father's legacy of fairness and honesty, while hiding behind an impenetrable armor of bureaucracy, legalisms and "civilization."

The fallout from the Walking Purchase seems to have permeated local scams and scandals down to the present. It's always been difficult for a Philadelphian to pick your pocket or sleep with your spouse without preaching you a sermon simultaneously.

When the British army occupied Philadelphia during the Revolution, Tory merchant Tench Coxe sold it delicacies at inflated prices while starving American prisoners fought over rats at the Walnut Street Jail. Fair enough—some of this country's wealthiest families started as privateers. But did Coxe have to pontificate, "If we must suffer misfortunes, let us drain all the good from them possible"?

Let's jump ahead to 1995 (we'll skip the 1970s and hippie guru Ira Einhorn, who lectured Philadelphia fat cats on love and peace while his girlfriend's corpse moldered in a trunk in his closet). That was the year the Ponzi scheme known as the Foundation for New Era Philanthropy went down in flames, after fleecing hundreds of local nonprofits, charities and schools of $135 million. Deeply regrettable. But my stomach didn't begin to churn until I read that New Era's founder, "Christian" businessman John G. Bennett Jr., planned to use possession by religious fervor as a legal defense.

Next to the self-righteous Bennett, Bernie Madoff's dead-eyed, tight-lipped, reptilian cold-bloodedness looks positively endearing.

But I'll let you start reading *Wicked Philadelphia* and see for yourself what William Penn's children hath wrought on their father's Holy Experiment. Why, I'll even wager that you'll find *Wicked Philadelphia* to be the most inspirational, uplifting book you've ever read. And if you don't find yourself spiritually transformed after you put it down, I'll pay you $100,000!

Of course, to claim your $100,000, you will need to submit a nonrefundable $5,000 processing fee to cover routine paperwork, taxes, shipping and handling. Just send your check, money order or cash (no coins or stamps, please) to Account No. XB15893Z42d, Bank of Antigua, 3708 Avenida de Contrahecho, St. John's, Antigua. You should receive your compensation within six to forty-eight months.

Trust me, gentle reader. Would I lie to you?

OH! IT'S A LOVELY WAR!

The Mischianza, 1778

> *Sir William he, snug as a flea,*
> *Lay all this time a snoring;*
> *Nor dream'd of harm as he lay warm*
> *In bed with Mrs. Loring.*
> —Francis Hopkinson, "The Battle of the Kegs"

On November 26, 1896, the social event of the Philadelphia season took place at Horticultural Hall, an elegant Italian palazzo next to the Academy of Music on South Broad Street. The cream of society gathered under the ballroom's coffered ceiling for the Mischianza Ball, named after a gala thrown by British officers for the city's belles during the American Revolution. The ball was the highlight of a four-day charity event that included, among its numerous attractions, a Wild West post office run by dainty debutantes in frontier attire, a play by the Mask & Wig Club of the University of Pennsylvania and a zodiac booth where Miss C. Dulaney Belt foretold the future.

Prince Louis of Savoy, grandson of King Victor Emmanuel II of Italy and guest of honor, arrived at the ball at 10:30 p.m. He was mobbed by would-be Cinderellas, who swarmed around the tall, handsome prince like bees on a honeycomb. Louis was rescued by Mrs. Edward Willing, glittering in her diamond tiara and necklace, for the grand march around the ballroom to inaugurate the evening. Behind the prince and Mrs. Willing came Mayor Charles F. Warwick, escorting Mrs. S. Weir Mitchell, wife of the renowned physician and author. They were followed by the ball's other patronesses and managers, members of Philadelphia's most aristocratic families, bearing names like Biddle, Cadwalader and Wharton.

After the grand march, couples took their places for a carefully choreographed quadrille. Young Samuel Chew II, dressed in a powdered wig and satin knee britches, escorted his sister Bessie (Elizabeth Oswald Chew), resplendent in her eighteenth-century silk ball gown, onto the dance floor. As the orchestra played, the handsome young couple gracefully executed an intricate minuet. Sam and Bessie were the youngest generation of a family that traced its American roots back to the seventeenth century. Their ancestors included Benjamin Chew, chief justice of the Supreme Court of the Province of Pennsylvania from 1775 to 1777. Since Benjamin's day, the Chews had lived at Cliveden, the colonial country house that still bore scars from the Battle of Germantown, fought in October 1777.

Tonight, Sam II was playing the role of John André, the British officer who had masterminded the original Mischianza in May 1778. Bessie was impersonating her ancestor Margaret ("Peggy") Chew, Benjamin's daughter and André's supposed sweetheart. As the couple concluded their dance, the audience applauded, enchanted by their youthful beauty and aristocratic grace. None of the guests was gauche enough to mention that American Patriots had cheered in 1780 when John André was hanged as a British spy or had cursed Peggy Chew as a treasonous harlot for consorting with the enemy.

The original Mischianza of May 1778 was the British army's swan song after a seven-month occupation of Philadelphia that had not only proved to be expensive and pointless but also had given its shattered enemy time to recover. No military force has ever celebrated its own ineptitude or acknowledged its own defeat with as much splendor and panache as the British army in the sunny spring of 1778.

When the British captured Philadelphia on September 26, 1777, they thought they had pierced the heart of the American rebellion. The city was the birthplace of the Declaration of Independence, seat of the Continental Congress and de facto capital of the United Colonies. They didn't realize that, unlike a traditional European power, the decentralized American government would not crumble once its capital was conquered. Congress quickly reassembled at York, and General Washington moved his forces to Valley Forge after the Battle of Germantown.

While American troops and civilians suffered through the bitter winter of 1777–78, the British hunkered down in relative luxury in Philadelphia.

Elizabeth Oswald Chew and Samuel Chew II dressed as Peggy Chew and John André for the 1896 Mischianza. *Courtesy of Cliveden, a National Trust Historic Site.*

General Sir William Howe, commander in chief of the British army in North America, occupied the mansion of former governor Richard Penn on Market Street below Sixth (later rebuilt as the President's House). Hessian commander Wilhelm Baron von Knyphausen claimed the John Cadwalader house on Second Street. Their officers commandeered other mansions, often displacing the owners to make room for their mistresses. Common soldiers had to be content at the almshouse, from which two hundred destitute adults and children were evicted in November 1777. Many of them later died from starvation and exposure.

Viewing himself as a "peace ambassador," Howe reached out to Philadelphia's upper classes during these dark days with receptions and parties. His officers entertained proper Philadelphians with plays at the Southwark Theatre and balls at Smith's Tavern. By diverting the elite, Howe hoped to win their hearts and minds, convincing them that they had stronger ties to the English aristocracy than to the noisy rabble demanding independence. Young ladies of quality—even those who called themselves Patriots—soon succumbed to the endless line of dashing young officers in well-cut red jackets.

Their parents usually supported the girls' fraternization. Many upper-class Philadelphians were staunch Loyalists who viewed the signers of the Declaration of Independence as traitors. Besides the Continental Congress, these Tories despised Pennsylvania's radical provincial government, which had undermined their political power by extending the vote to all tax-paying free men. Other Philadelphians—later known as neutralists—enjoyed Howe's hospitality but remained discreet, waiting to see which way the wind would blow.

Howe's aide-de-camp in his dance-card diplomacy was Captain John André, a handsome, charming combination of soldier and social secretary. André established himself in the house of Benjamin Franklin, then seeking the support of the French monarchy at Versailles. To occupy himself in his ample free time, André penned verses, acted in plays, painted watercolors and made love to the prettiest girls in town. His favorites were the two Peggys: Peggy Chew, daughter of Benjamin Chew, and Peggy Shippen, daughter of neutralist Judge Edward Shippen.

Throughout the bleak winter, Howe focused on his duties as peace ambassador, making no effort to pursue his decimated enemy twenty miles away. The tall, heavy, coarse-featured general, cool and fearless in combat, was "the most indolent of mortals" off the battlefield according to American general Charles Lee. Even after spring arrived, Howe busied himself in Philadelphia with his mistress, Elizabeth Loring (wife of his commissary general of military prisoners), while General Washington and Baron von Steuben rebuilt the American army at Valley Forge. In France, Benjamin Franklin noted that "Philadelphia has taken Howe."

In May 1778, Howe was replaced as commander in chief by General Sir Henry Clinton and summoned home to London to justify his lackluster performance before his critics in Parliament. Before he left, his loyal officers decided to throw him the farewell party to end all parties. Twenty-two of them passed the tricorn hat and raised 3,312 guineas, a sum that would have supported the American army for a week. Adjusted for simple inflation, 3,312 guineas equal $577,776 today; adjusted to reflect the growth in workers' earnings since 1778, the sum jumps to $7,384,609. Either way, this purse was more than enough to underwrite an unforgettable blowout.

John André took charge as artistic director, supported by a small cadre of equally aesthetic officers. Together, they planned an event called the Mischianza (sometimes spelled Meschianza), an Italian term meaning "medley" or "miscellany." André himself crafted the invitation, a laurel-bordered cartouche supported by cannons, flags and other military accoutrements. While the cartouche showed a setting sun, its legend asserted, "*Luceo discedens aucto splendore resurgam*" ("I shine in descent but shall rise again in greater splendor"). Hundreds of invitations were sent to Philadelphia's first families, many of whom accepted with delight. Meanwhile, dozens of British soldiers were assigned to erect temporary structures at an abandoned estate south of the city.

On May 18, 1778, a warm and sunny Monday, elegant carriages choked Knight's Wharf at Green Street in Northern Liberties, where the

Mischianza's four hundred participants boarded flatboats. At 4:00 p.m., three boats filled with musicians cast off from the wharf, leading an imperial waterborne procession down the Delaware. In a lavishly decorated galley behind them, General Sir William Howe sat in state, accompanied by his brother Admiral Sir Richard Howe, his successor General Sir Henry Clinton, his mistress Mrs. Loring and his retinue of officers and ladies. Two other galleys and a string of barges carried the other celebrants. Cannons boomed as British warships in the harbor hailed their commanders. Spectators filled dozens of smaller boats that bobbed among the larger vessels and packed every wharf and rooftop overlooking the Delaware. While some cheered the spectacle, others cursed the grandiose display.

The regatta landed at the Association Battery at the foot of what is now Wharton Street, where it was saluted by nineteen guns from two warships. A military band preceded the assemblage, led by the Howes, up the sloping lawn of Walnut Grove, country seat of the late Joseph Wharton (at current-day Wharton and Fifth Streets). Two rows of towering grenadiers and light-horsemen, in full uniform and at stiff attention, lined the path of the procession from the river to the estate.

As the celebrants approached the mansion, they passed under a triumphal arch honoring Admiral Howe, decorated with naval trophies and topped by Neptune with his trident. One hundred yards farther on, they passed through a second arch honoring General Howe, adorned with military trophies and surmounted by a figure of Fame. Between the arches, two temporary pavilions faced each other, forming a rectangular arena for the afternoon's diversions.

The first row of seats in each pavilion was reserved for the fourteen Ladies of the Mischianza, "the foremost in youth, beauty and fashion," with seven sitting on each side. They wore costumes designed by André in a stylized Turkish fashion popular in London: sheer robes of flowing white silk with sashes tied in a large bow and tall gauze turbans covered with feathers and pearls. The outfits of the ladies in one pavilion were trimmed in white and rose, while those in the opposite pavilion bore touches of black and orange. These ladies were the daughters of the city's most elite families: Chew, Bond, Redman, Franks, White, Smith, Craig and, possibly, Shippen.

One of the mysteries of the Mischianza is whether Peggy Shippen and her two sisters, Mary and Sarah, actually attended. Their names appear in some accounts, and one of Sarah Shippen's granddaughters insisted that her grandmother loved to recall the event. But other family chronicles assert that Edward Shippen forbade his three daughters from going at the

A Knight of the Blended Rose, with herald and page, as drawn by Mischianza organizer John André. *Courtesy of Cliveden, a National Trust Historic Site.*

last moment. While the official reason given is that he was ashamed of their flimsy costumes, it's more likely that the neutralist judge had detected a shift in the wind. Rumors were circulating that the British would soon desert Philadelphia.

Once the guests were seated, a flourish of trumpets announced the Ceremony of the Carousel, a fairy-tale joust. Seven knights on white horses rode into the enclosure. They looked like musketeers in their pink-and-white satin costumes inspired by the French court of Henry IV, with baggy trousers, puffed sleeves and plumed hats. Their herald carried a shield showing a white rose entwined with a red rose and the motto "We droop when separated." These were the Knights of the Blended Rose, who saluted the pink-and-white damsels and issued a challenge that no other ladies equaled them in "Wit, Beauty, and every Accomplishment." Among them was John André, who swore his fealty to Miss Peggy Chew.

In response, seven knights on black horses charged into the enclosure, dressed in black-and-orange versions of the same outfit. These were the

Knights of the Burning Mountain, whose herald bore a shield with an erupting volcano and the motto "I burn for ever." The black knights saluted their ladies in the opposite pavilion and accepted the challenge to defend their honor, and the tournament began. After several playful passes on horseback with lance, pistol and sword that harmed no one, the marshal of the field declared a tie, deeming "the Ladies so fair and the Knights so brave that it would have been impious to decide in favor of either."

Evening was falling, and the Mischianza guests strolled through formal gardens to the Wharton mansion for refreshments and cards. Over one door of the gaming room stood a painting of a cornucopia filled with flowers, while over the opposite door was a second cornucopia, empty and withered. These were ominous emblems for the gambling-mad British: several officers lost everything that evening, including their military commissions, and returned to England bankrupt and disgraced.

After cards, the company proceeded to the ballroom. The blue, pink and gold walls of the vast chamber were lined with eighty-five tall mirrors and thirty-four candelabra borrowed from local residents, creating an illusion of infinite space and brilliance. The knights and their ladies opened the ball with a minuet. At 9:00 p.m., the music stopped, and guests crowded

A somewhat inaccurate nineteenth-century depiction of the Mischianza tournament, from Watson's *Annals*. The knights were dressed in French Renaissance style rather than in medieval armor.

around the windows to view fireworks. As cascades of light filled the sky, General Howe's triumphal arch burst into life, spouting Chinese fountains and rockets. The figure of Fame sparkled with stars, and a fiery banner emerged from her trumpet with the French motto *Tes lauriers sont immortels* (your laurels are immortal).

Not all of the noise was produced by fireworks. Some explosions came from British cannons defending the redoubts north of the city against an attack by American commandos. For a brief moment, reality threatened to crash the party, until the British instructed their musicians to play more loudly and drown out the cannon fire.

Supper was announced at midnight, when a seemingly solid wall composed of folding doors melted away to reveal a vast dining saloon, ablaze with dozens more mirrors and candelabra. Black servants in turbans and sashes greeted the celebrants with a low salaam before serving them an opulent banquet of twelve hundred dishes.

Refreshed by this snack, the guests returned to the ballroom and danced until dawn, when the long party finally ground to a halt. The ladies were escorted home by British officers, who retreated to coffeehouses and taverns to fortify themselves for the coming day. Back at Walnut Grove, soldiers began to dismantle André's artifice and to return the mirrors and candelabra to their owners.

The Mischianza's fourteen hours of illusion were followed by a long hangover. On the evening of May 19, General Howe led nearly twelve thousand British troops to Barren Hill northwest of the city, hoping to capture twenty-two hundred American forces led by the Marquis de Lafayette. Thanks to advance warning—and perhaps the party-pooped British officers—Lafayette was able to lead his troops from under the enemy's nose to safety across the Schuylkill, with only a few casualties. Howe's final attempt to secure a military victory in America had failed.

Five days later, Sir William Howe sailed for England to face his critics. The Mischianza, which his officers hoped would demonstrate their loyalty, was denounced by English Whigs after a narrative of the event, penned by the publicity-hungry André, appeared in London's *Gentleman's Magazine*. Despite these attacks, Howe was fully exonerated, later becoming a powerful political figure. At his death in 1814, the Fifth Viscount Howe was a privy counselor to the British Crown and governor of Plymouth.

The day after Howe's departure, British officials informed Joseph Galloway, civilian superintendent general of police, that their army would leave Philadelphia within the month. France had entered the war as an

American ally in February, and Clinton wanted to concentrate his forces in British-held New York.

Many Tories panicked at news of the impending evacuation, fearful of partisan retribution. One witness described "a Continual scene of Terror, Hurry & Confusion," while another reported that "nothing but misery & Sorrow are to be seen in the Town." The preoccupied Clinton was besieged by desperate Loyalists, begging for protection. Meanwhile, merchants who had eagerly extended credit now pleaded for payment from British officers, who viewed settling their debts as an extremely low priority. The departing army would leave over £10,000 in unpaid bills.

In early June, the Delaware River was jammed with nearly three hundred ships to transport three thousand Tory refugees to New York or London. Streets surrounding the harbor were crowded with carts and wagons filled with Loyalists' possessions, most of which would be left on the wharves or dumped into the Delaware. Once the transports were loaded, they sailed forty-five miles south of Philadelphia, where they sat moored for two weeks while Clinton prepared his troops. The immobilized ships were packed with despairing refugees, living in filthy conditions on meager rations as they waited for the signal to sail. Among them was Rebecca Franks, one of the belles of the Mischianza, who would marry a British officer and die in London as Lady Johnson in 1823.

One month after the Mischianza, Clinton's seventeen thousand British troops evacuated Philadelphia. From June 15 to June 18, flatboats ferried men, horses, artillery, wagons and provisions across the Delaware to Cooper's Point (Camden), from whence they proceeded overland across New Jersey to New York City. Lieutenant John André's luggage included books, musical instruments, scientific equipment and a portrait of Benjamin Franklin, all of which he had looted from Franklin's house (the portrait was returned in 1906 and now hangs in the White House). At the same time, the moored fleet was given its signal to disembark and transported its cargo of refugees to safety in New York or London.

Less than fifteen minutes after the last British left Philadelphia on June 18, the first American soldiers entered the ruined city. In the following days, mobs attacked a few Tories, but General Benedict Arnold, military commander of the city, limited violence by declaring martial law. Councils of Safety, composed of radical Patriots, seized Tory property and ordered Loyalists to report for trial. The estates of seventy-nine Philadelphians were confiscated, and over one hundred were convicted of treason. Three of them were executed.

The Ladies of the Mischianza were not placed on trial. Some Philadelphians tried to shun or censor them for socializing with the enemy. When Washington's officers planned a ball to honor French officers who had assisted their cause, there was talk of excluding those Mischianza maidens still in Philadelphia. But their wealthy and prominent families were now official Patriots, and the girls received invitations.

Of the eleven women who were definitely at the Mischianza, two besides Rebecca Franks moved to England. Most of the others married wealthy and prominent Americans and became members of the country's new republican aristocracy. In 1779, Peggy Shippen married General Benedict Arnold. Peggy Chew married Colonel John Eager Howard of Maryland, although she kept a place in her heart for her Mischianza knight. Years later, Mrs. Howard told a visitor to her Baltimore home that "Major André was a most witty and cultivated gentleman." Her husband, who had fought Howe's forces at White Plains and Monmouth, thundered, "He was a damned spy, sir; nothing but a damned spy!"

John André, the impresario of the Mischianza, did become a spy. After leaving Philadelphia, he was promoted to the rank of major and placed in charge of British Secret Intelligence. Tories put him in touch with Benedict Arnold, who needed money and was unhappy with his treatment by Congress. The two men plotted for Arnold, then commander of West Point, to surrender the crucial garrison to the British, giving them control of the Hudson Valley. Historians believe that Peggy Shippen Arnold knew of the conspiracy, although the extent of her involvement is uncertain.

On September 23, 1780, André was captured by American militiamen after conferring with Benedict Arnold at West Point. When they searched him, they found documents from Arnold describing the plot. Tipped off, the Arnolds were able to escape to British-held New York. In 1782, they moved to London, where they would spend the rest of their lives, while Arnold's name became an American synonym for "traitor."

George Washington turned down André's request for a firing squad, the proper mode of execution for an officer and a gentleman. On October 2, 1780, the thirty-year-old spy was hanged like a common criminal in Tappan, New York, and his body buried in a plain coffin under the gallows. In 1821, the Duke of York had André's remains transferred to the Hero's Corner of Westminster Abbey and placed beneath a magnificent monument depicting a sorrowful Britannia. The elderly Mrs. Benedict Arnold was a frequent visitor to his tomb.

Forgotten after the Revolution, the Mischianza was reborn as a literary phenomenon in the 1800s, thanks to writers like George Lippard, Washington Irving and S. Weir Mitchell. The earlier books, written during America's formative years, stress British decadence and indolence versus native rectitude and self-sacrifice. But after the Civil War, attitudes toward Great Britain softened, and upper-class Americans delighted in Anglophilia. In Henry Peterson's *Pemberton* (1873), the Mischianza is lauded as "the finest and most artistic entertainment in the way of a festivity, that ever delighted the eyes of beautiful women and brave men in this prosaic American world."

In 1894, Sophie Howard Ward, great-granddaughter of Peggy Chew, fueled interest in the Mischianza when she published John André's narrative of the event in *Century Illustrated* magazine. The memoir, illustrated with André's watercolors, had been presented to Peggy Chew by her admiring knight shortly before his departure in June 1778. After publication, Ward sold the original manuscript to her cousins, "Centennial" Sam and Mary Johnson Chew, owners of Cliveden and parents of Sam II and Bessie.

Two years later, under the Chews' guidance, the Mischianza became an opportunity for America's elite to mingle with European nobles like the Prince of Savoy, la Comtesse de Diesbach and the Countess Pappenheim (née Mary Wheeler of Philadelphia, having purchased her husband and title with a multimillion-dollar dowry).

As John André and Peggy Chew danced in Horticultural Hall, the vulgar Vanity Fair of the previous century was reborn as a celebration of gentility and elegance, where the pure-blooded aristocracies of two great nations joined hands. With one minuet, the traitors of 1778 had been transformed into the transatlantic trendsetters of 1896.

BROTHERLY LOVE AND
SISTERLY AFFECTION

The Rise of the Red Light Districts, circa 1820

Times are much changed, and maids are become mistresses.
—Elizabeth Drinker, December 18, 1778

On August 12, 1800, the concerned citizens of Southwark decided to improve property values in their neighborhood by torching a large chunk of it. That night, an angry mob burned down the China Factory, a notorious brothel on China (now Alter) Street between Front and Second. Originally, the cluster of brick and wooden buildings near the Delaware River had housed the American China Manufactory, founded in 1770 as one of the first porcelain works in the New World. Although the enterprise failed after two years, its name stuck when the site became a cannon foundry during the Revolution.

But by 1800, the China Factory had degenerated into one of the region's most notorious whorehouses, popular with sailors, apprentices and clerks. Many of the decent families who lived nearby were disgusted by its incessant noise, foul language and brawls, not to mention the blatant carnality that often occurred in broad daylight. They complained frequently to the police, who remained oblivious, thanks to bribes from the brothel's proprietors.

In August, a death at the China Factory brought matters to a head. Two of its patrons—a young block maker (who carved the wooden type blocks used in a printer's press) and the petty officer of a warship—got into a fistfight. Their respective "mistresses," along with other patrons and prostitutes, cheered the fighters on. Finally, the block maker collapsed and was carried away, to die from his beating twelve hours later. The boatswain was arrested and charged with manslaughter.

Soon after, local residents burned and dismantled the China Factory, a process that took two days. By the time they were through, only the chimneys remained of the six buildings that had once contained the brothel. Although some rioters were arrested, public sympathy was on their side. A newspaper reported that

> the buildings which have been destroy'd, were, for a long time, the subject of regret by the well-disposed Citizens of Southwark; and the eagerness with which this opportunity was seized for their destruction is sufficient proof of the detestation in which their infamous occupants was held by the public.

Elizabeth Drinker, matriarch of a prominent Quaker family, copied out the entire article in her diary, since "I was pleased to hear that such Creatures were routed—I am not pleas'd to hear of riots and could wish that a more justifiable power had taken them in hand long ago. 'Tis a shame to our police that any such houses is suffer'd."

The destruction of the China Factory marked the first breezes of a sea change in the practice of the oldest profession in Philadelphia. During the eighteenth century, prostitution was an accepted part of life in the Quaker City. If not condoned, it was widely tolerated and integrated into every neighborhood and social class.

But during the nineteenth century, the gathering storm of Victorian morality swept most brothels into "vice zones" outside respectable neighborhoods. The same indignation created a moral gulf, as well as a geographical one, between the prostitute and polite society. Reform groups sprang up to rescue fallen women from a fate worse than death and restore them to respectability. Perversely, the physical and ethical segregation of prostitution helped it to blossom from a cottage industry to a growth sector by the Civil War.

Prostitutes might have been operating in Philadelphia before William Penn arrived in 1682. If not, they set up shop soon afterward. As the town's original settlers constructed houses, their abandoned caves along the Delaware (usually cabins or huts built into the soft earth of the riverbank) were used as unlicensed taverns, gambling dens and brothels. Back in England, Penn ordered the provincial council to evict the evildoers after receiving reports of their troglodytic transgressions. Between 1685 and 1690, the caves were

High Street Market, a center of prostitution in Philadelphia. At left, drunken sailors stagger, and a gentleman and girl appear to be striking a bargain.

demolished, allowing Penn to lease his riverfront property to developers and to "let virtue be cherisht."

In the eighteenth century, the busiest area for "strollers" or streetwalkers remained the waterfront. Dozens of ships docked at Philadelphia's wharves every day, filled with sailors who had not seen a woman for weeks. They patronized prostitutes who were often the wives or widows of sailors, struggling to survive during their husbands' long or permanent absences. These women took their johns back to rented rooms at disreputable inns or taverns like the Three Mariners or serviced them outdoors, in one of the innumerable alleys or courtyards near the docks.

Other prostitutes frequented the open-air market sheds that extended west from Second Street along the middle of High Street, targeting the provincial farmers who sold their produce every Wednesday and Saturday. In 1794, Margaret Britton was arrested for "skulking about Country Waggons in High Street at a late Hour of the Night, and acknowledges that she wished to have carnal Intercourse with them to get money." Some women stationed themselves along the major roads leading out of the city—Baltimore, Germantown and Lancaster Pikes—to waylay farmers in need of a little relaxation on their journeys home.

After the Revolution, Philadelphia became the political and economic center of the United States, serving as the country's national capital between 1790 and 1800. Many social historians now view this period as an era of both political and sexual liberation. In the overcrowded, heterogeneous city, described by one historian as "boisterous and bawdy," relations between the different races, sexes and classes were relaxed and fluid. Flush with government spending and filled with founding fathers far away from their founding mothers, the metropolis was poised to become America's first great party town. What happened in Philadelphia stayed in Philadelphia.

Thomas Mifflin, governor of Pennsylvania from 1790 to 1799, "lived in a state of adultery with many women during the life of his wife," causing the poor woman to die from a broken heart. William Wister, a wealthy Quaker merchant, was footing the bill for four different mistresses when he died in 1801. Since Wister had the poor taste to die in one of their houses, the Quakers refused to let him be laid to rest in their burial ground. But the more liberal Baptists were happy to accept his corpse.

Prostitution flourished in freewheeling Philadelphia. One visitor remarked on the numerous "ladies of pleasure" who flooded the streets at night. The *Philadelphiad*, a satirical poem published in 1784, catalogued the landmarks of the raucous city, including the State House, courthouse, jailhouse and *bagnio* (a classy Italian word for "whorehouse"). Among the bagnio's clients was a religious hypocrite who was "always preaching morals," despite being known "to every old procuress in the town." He might have been inspired by John Hay, a once-respected minister who abandoned his family to live in sin with a parishioner.

In a city where a worker's wooden hovel might abut a marble mansion, brothels were everywhere. While no reliable statistics exist, they probably numbered in the hundreds. Some districts, like Southwark, had a higher concentration of brothels. But bordellos operated in the most fashionable neighborhoods. When General Thaddeus Kosciuszko, hero of the Revolution, returned to Philadelphia in 1797 as a political exile from Poland, he lodged at Mrs. Sarah Lawson's boardinghouse at 7 South Fourth Street. Although Mrs. Lawson's establishment was perfectly respectable, it stood in the middle of an early red-light district.

Official attempts to eradicate this social evil were sparse since, in the words of one observer, "the municipal police connive at this sort of house." According to historian Clare A. Lyons, there were only 53 arrests in Philadelphia for prostitution during its ten years as the nation's capital, plus 142 arrests for vagrancy (a charge usually meant to remove disorderly women from the street). Criminal prosecutions against prostitutes or brothel owners were rare, since the law required witnesses to testify against them. Not surprisingly, many of those who could provide evidence chose not to. Meanwhile, madams and prostitutes often sued their customers for nonpayment, assault and battery or drunk and disorderly conduct.

With the dawning of the nineteenth century, the blatant sexual energy of the previous era began to dissipate. The American republic was taking shape, and its inhabitants tried to emulate the early Roman virtues of hard work, familial devotion and religious piety. Philadelphia, no longer the capital of either the United States or Pennsylvania, saw both its expendable income and self-esteem shrink. As the city's prosperity was threatened by new hostilities with Britain and competition from Baltimore and New York, businessmen felt compelled to spend more time in the countinghouse and less in the whorehouse.

Gradually, citizens joined forces with the municipal authorities to attack this social evil with a combination of reform and repression. During this period, the number of arrests and prosecutions for prostitution and brothel-keeping began to increase, as did the severity of fines and prison terms. These trends would continue throughout the nineteenth century.

In response, most brothels moved from the center of town to outlying areas where they could attract customers yet avoid official attention. The traditional vice zone of Southwark flourished, expanding north to absorb the African American enclave on South and Bainbridge Streets east of Eighth. While the China Factory was gone, Southwark still boasted Dandy Hall on Plum Alley, a combination brothel/dance hall/gambling den/hotel. In neighboring Moyamensing, Duffy's Arcade was the "Astor House of the Underworld." Its numerous eight- by ten-foot rooms, each illuminated only by a square sawed in its wooden door, could be rented by the hour.

Besides Southwark and Moyamensing, several new red-light districts emerged in the early nineteenth century. The notorious Seventh Ward, another predominantly African American district, extended from Spruce to South Street and from Seventh to the Schuylkill River, with a heavy concentration of brothels around Twelfth and Pine. The Tenderloin was bounded approximately by Callowhill and Race Streets and by Sixth and Broad. Within it, there were clusters of brothels at Eleventh and Wood Streets and in the area northwest of Franklin Square known as Skid Row. The Northern Liberties, which became an industrial district during this time, extended from Vine Street to Girard Avenue and from Fifth Street to the Delaware River.

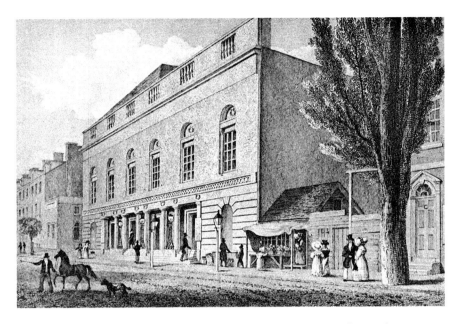

The Walnut Street Theatre. Another popular spot for prostitutes, who disrupted performances by standing on benches and waving at prospective johns in the galleries.

The inhabitants of these areas—poor African Americans, foreign immigrants and workers—had little power. They were at the mercy of the brothel owners, who could bribe local police and officials. At the same time, these red-light districts were easily accessible to the "better sort." A Rittenhouse Square resident could stop by Twelfth and Pine after leaving his office on lower Chestnut Street and still be home in time for dinner.

Despite this segregation, some streetwalkers—identifiable by their revealing calico dresses, bright jewelry and uncovered heads—continued to canvass the city. In 1841, two strollers were arrested after soliciting Mayor John Swift and his friend on Walnut Street. Other prostitutes drummed up business in the theatres, where they often disrupted performances by standing on benches to wave to their male friends in the galleries. In 1836, a grand jury charged the Walnut Street Theatre with being a public nuisance because of the soliciting there.

To protect upper-class gentlemen from harm on their nocturnal forays, an unknown Samaritan compiled a Baedeker for bordellos. *A Guide to the Stranger, or Pocket Companion for The Fancy, Containing a List of the Gay Houses and Ladies of Pleasure in the City of Brotherly Love and Sisterly Affection* (an extremely misleading title to modern readers) was published in 1849. The *Guide* rated nearly fifty individual brothels, bed houses (where streetwalkers could rent rooms) and houses of assignation (where married women could meet their lovers or where rakes could lure young virgins to their ruin).

The anonymous author emphasized that the *Guide* was meant to shield strangers and "our gay city larks" from "the snares employed by the wily courtesans"; that is, to help them avoid being infected, robbed, beaten or murdered. "With this book in hand," the author promised, "a man will be enabled to shun those low dens of infamy and disease with which this city abounds."

The *Guide* embodied the social and racial prejudices of its era. The best parlor-houses, "frequented only by gentlemen," were parodies of upper-class homes. Madams were dignified and maternally attentive to their visitors. Prostitutes were well-dressed, well-mannered white girls whose gifts included playing the piano, singing and polite conversation. Whatever their talents upstairs, downstairs these damsels were almost as ladylike as their customers' wives and sisters.

Meanwhile, the *Guide* warned its readers about a brothel on South Street above Eighth, "occupied by a swarm of yellow girls" who "strange to say, meet with more custom than their fairer skinned rivals." The author sneered that he had "no objection to a white man hugging a negro wench to his bosom, providing his stomach is strong enough to relish the infliction."

Houses where "a single visit might be the cause of utter ruin and disgrace" were indicated by an X. Among these dens was Mrs. Hamilton's house, on Locust between Tenth and Eleventh. Mrs. Hamilton, the *Guide* warned, had been in business long enough "that she has grown bald and toothless in the service. Beware of this house, stranger, as you would the sting of a viper."

Surprisingly, no X marks the entry for Sal Boyer, alias Dutch Sal, described as "the lowest house in the city…worse than hell itself." Sal ran a panel house, where sliding walls enabled her to steal valuables from the discarded clothes of gentlemen otherwise engaged. But her ultimate sin in the *Guide*'s eyes was having "connection with the lowest negro, for the small remuneration of potatoes and flour to support her boarders!" Evidently, Sal's infamy was citywide, since no address was given for her hellhole.

At the other end of the spectrum were the sophisticated sirens of Wood Street in the Tenderloin. Miss Sarah Turner at No. 2 Wood was "a perfect Queen," employing four "young, beautiful, and enchanting creatures" who played the piano and sang. "None but gentlemen visit this Paradise of Love," the *Guide* assured its discriminating readers. Miss Mary Blessington, at No. 3, was "as snug a lump of flesh and blood as ever man pressed to his bosom." At No. 4 Wood, the accomplished Josephine Somers ran "a Temple of Venus. Go one, go all, and you will be pleased," the *Guide* exhorted.

Other houses received only one star due to their lack of distinction. On Blackberry Alley, Ann Carson ran a "genteel loafer crib, not frequented by those having pretensions to respectability." The landlady of My Pretty Jane, at Pine and Quince Streets, was "a well disposed woman, but her ideas are not elevated enough"—meaning she hadn't read Emerson?—"consequently her shanty is the resort of very common people."

While respectable gentlemen, clutching the *Guide* in their sweaty palms, ventured into Philadelphia's red-light districts in search of pleasure, respectable ladies were venturing there to save prostitutes from disease and degradation. Some *filles de joie* might have received separate visits from both a husband and his wife, each with a different purpose in mind, during the same twenty-four-hour period.

By 1850, Philadelphia had two organizations dedicated to rescuing the city's estimated six thousand prostitutes from sin and restoring them to polite society in acceptably subservient roles: the Magdalen Society and the Rosine Association. A third organization, the Female Moral Reform Society, tried to identify and ostracize the "licentious men" who frequented prostitutes. It did not flourish, as its members encountered "a coldness and indifference, and in some cases, hostility," from many prominent Philadelphians who worried that they might be on the group's hit list.

In 1807, the Magdalen Society bought the western end of the block bordered by Twentieth, Race, Twenty-first and Winter Streets (now occupied by the Franklin Institute). There, they built a "Home for Magdalens" to house about a dozen fallen women, replacing it with a larger brick building in the 1840s. This rural retreat, far outside the city, was meant to protect its inmates from society and vice versa. According to one contemporary observer, "If reformation is an effect of solitude, the building and grounds are well suited to effect the purpose."

Behind a thirteen-foot brick wall topped by spikes, life inside the "Magdalen Prison" was grim. A new inmate was literally and figuratively stripped of her former identity. Upon her arrival, she was led through a confusing maze of entries and corridors, symbolizing the doors she was closing on her old life. Once she had arrived at her cell deep within the building, her clothing was replaced by a drab uniform and her name by a number. Her days were filled with religious training and work. She had limited contact with the staff and other inmates, similar to Eastern State

Penitentiary prisoners kept in solitary confinement. Needless to say, most of the prostitutes who asked for admittance were aging, sick or destitute, with no other options.

In 1847, women from various churches formed the Rosine Association for "the reformation, employment, and instruction of females who had led immoral lives." These women wished to provide more sympathetic care than the Magdalen Society, under the auspices of an organization that they controlled (as opposed to Magdalen's all-male board of trustees). They acknowledged that many brothel customers were "the husbands, the fathers, the brothers, and the sons of virtuous women in our community."

Instead of isolating its wards, the Rosine Association purchased a fourteen-room "house of industry" on Eighth Street above Wood in the heart of the Tenderloin. To drum up business, the gentlewomen canvassed the district, making 160 visits to brothels during their first six months of operation. They discovered that a single block in the Tenderloin might hold thirteen or fourteen bordellos.

Understanding that many women were forced into prostitution out of financial need, the Rosine Association taught its wards how to sew, weave and make clothing. Women could choose their trade and were paid for their labors, providing them with a bankroll upon their release. Inmates were also instructed in reading, writing, arithmetic, grammar, geography, physiology and the Bible and were even treated to occasional "intervals of recreation." At the end of their first year, the Rosine Association had taken in twenty-five women. Seven were placed with respectable families as servants, four were sent home to their own families, one was married to the man "who had induced her to err," two went to the almshouse for health reasons, two left voluntarily and one incorrigible case was asked to leave.

While the Magdalen Society and Rosine Association helped hundreds of women, they were ultimately powerless to stop the spread of prostitution in Philadelphia. For every woman who requested admission, there were one hundred who could not or would not enter. Meanwhile, the number of prostitutes continued to grow, as girls and women were pushed into the profession through desertion, entrapment, pregnancy, widowhood, divorce, rape or simple poverty.

Although no official statistics were kept, it's safe to say that recidivism rates were high for alumnae of the Magdalen and Rosine asylums. Even the trustees of the Magdalen Society had to admit that less than one-third of its inmates turned over a new leaf. Much of the problem was simple economics: a moderately successful prostitute might earn more in one hour than the dollar she would be paid for a week's labor at an asylum. Training for a "respectable" life as a servant or seamstress was no guarantee against poverty. For decades to come, the financial vicissitudes of being a single female would force many women into selling their bodies to survive.

Other women may have decided to take their chances on the streets or in a brothel, preferring (in the words of a Rosine Association annual report) "the exhilarating glass, the exciting game of cards, the profuse expenditure of money" to the austere security of an asylum. Maybe they simply wanted the right to wear their own clothes, sleep late on a Sunday or be called by their proper names. With the perverse willfulness that characterizes human beings, they may have valued their own independence, however hazardous, over the docile obedience demanded by their respectable saviors. For many of Philadelphia's fallen women, it was a far better fate to be a queen in hell than a servant in heaven.

THE VICTORIANS CALLED IT "SEDUCTION"

The Heberton-Mercer Murder Case, 1843

"Then," said I, "Philadelphia is not so pure as it looks?"
"Alas, alas, that I should have to say it," said the old man with an expression
of deep sorrow, "but whenever I behold its regular streets and formal look, I
think of The Whited Sepulchre, without all purity, within, all rottenness and
dead men's bones."
　　　　　　　　　　　　　　　—*George Lippard,* The Quaker City,
　　　　　　　　　　　　　　　　　　or, the Monks of Monk Hall

Friday, February 10, 1843, was a bitterly cold night in Philadelphia. Although little snow had fallen, the Delaware River had begun to freeze, and iceboats struggled to keep the busy port open for business. Massive merchant vessels, their masts as tall as a ten-story building, crept along the icy channel, heading south to the Atlantic. Small steamboats chugged back and forth across the river, ferrying goods and passengers between Philadelphia and Camden.

A few blocks west, the bell in the tower of Independence Hall (which most Philadelphians still called the Old State House) struck five o'clock. At Fifth and Walnut, a young man hid in the shadows and watched one of the brick row houses on the south side of Walnut. A carriage laden with luggage turned up a narrow alley in the middle of the block. Two men emerged from the side of the house and hurried into the carriage, which turned around and headed east. The young man hailed a cab.

"Follow that carriage," he commanded the startled driver. "Drive like the devil. Go to hell after it, if it goes there!"

Sin in the City of Brotherly Love

It was dark when the two carriages reached the Market Street wharf on the Delaware River, where a few pedestrians and a horse-drawn coal wagon waited to board the steamboat *John Fitch* for Camden. The first carriage clambered onto the ferry. The young man paid his cab and boarded the steamboat on foot, standing behind the coal wagon, which had stopped across the deck from the carriage.

Shortly after 5:30 p.m. a whistle blew. The *John Fitch* lurched away from the dock, its side wheels churning as plumes of black smoke erupted from the twin funnels near its bow. The horses harnessed to the carriage and coal wagon shied and whinnied at the commotion but calmed down as the ship assumed a steady pace. The young man held his breath as the carriage door opened and a gentleman in his mid-twenties emerged, wearing a tall beaver hat and a heavy overcoat. The young man hid behind the wagon as Beaver Hat strolled around, peering at the faces of his fellow passengers, before returning to his vehicle.

A few minutes later, the steamboat passed through the narrow channel at the northern end of Windmill Island, dug to create a straight passage between Philadelphia and Camden. The canal was icy, and the horses grew restless as the steamboat bumped against the floes. The carriage driver climbed down from his box and stood next to one horse, calming it. Beaver Hat left the carriage again and took the bridle of the other animal.

Soon the lights of Camden came into view. The *John Fitch* shuddered as it glided into the Federal Street wharf. Beaver Hat and the driver were preoccupied at the front of the carriage, soothing the jittery horses. Passengers gathered their possessions and pushed forward, preparing to debark. In the confusion, the young man emerged from behind the coal wagon. He strode across the deck to the carriage, thrust a pistol through the rear window curtain and fired four shots blindly. Panicked by the noise, the horses reared and whinnied, while other passengers screamed and scurried for safety.

Beaver Hat ran back and flung open the carriage door. Inside, his companion lay crumpled on the floor, groaning but barely conscious, as a pool of blood spread beneath him. The man shut the door and grabbed the shooter's arm, muttering, "This is a pretty piece of business."

Later, everyone recounted a different version of how the young man had behaved after the shooting. Some remembered him as deadly calm, surrendering his pistol without a struggle. Some said he declaimed dramatically, "The deed is done! I give myself up to justice." Still others recalled him laughing maniacally and calling for a fiddle so that all could dance. Only one thing was certain: Singleton Mercer had just killed Mahlon Hutchinson Heberton, the alleged rapist of Mercer's sixteen-year-old sister.

The murder was the denouement of a scandal that had titillated Philadelphia for nearly a week. On the morning of February 6, young Sarah Mercer had left her family residence at 33 Queen Street in Southwark and disappeared for two days. Her father, Thomas, a wealthy retired merchant and a leader in the Presbyterian Church, was deeply worried. Sarah was only sixteen and very pretty but was also described as "childlike" and "of rather weak intellect." Thomas Mercer's anxiety increased when rumors spread that Sarah had eloped with, or had been abducted by, twenty-four-year-old Mahlon Hutchinson Heberton, the socially prominent son of the late Dr. John C. Heberton.

Many Philadelphians considered Heberton to be the epitome of the wild young man known as a "sport," who patronized the city's billiard halls, bowling alleys and bordellos. The *Spirit of the Times*, a populist newspaper, described him as "rather tall, extremely well formed, remarkably full in the chest, was always dressed in the extreme of the fashion (corseted, padded, etc., to a nicety), had dark hair, a brilliant and rakish eye, wore a moustache, and carried a gold-headed cane." The *Spirit* revealed that Heberton had spent most of his inheritance and was considered a "lady-killer." The *Public Ledger*, a penny paper popular with workers, disclosed that Heberton "bore the character of a roué, and boasted of his success with the women."

On February 8, Thomas Mercer had Heberton arrested and taken to the office of the local alderman. Heberton swore that he knew nothing of Sarah's whereabouts. He did deign to inform her twenty-three-year-old brother Singleton that "there was a girl came near our house last night, and when someone went to the door she ran away. She looked enough like you to be your sister." When Thomas Mercer begged Heberton to restore his daughter's reputation with an offer of marriage, the sport refused. Sarah, child of an Irish immigrant tradesman, was Heberton's social inferior, regardless of her father's wealth. With no evidence and no confession, the alderman was obliged to release Heberton, despite the Mercers' indignation.

Meanwhile, Sarah's mother, Eliza, visited Ann Heberton, Mahlon's widowed mother, at her home on North Ninth Street above Arch and begged her to persuade her son to return Sarah. The bemused Mrs. Heberton was unable to help. When Singleton subsequently challenged Heberton to a duel, the latter declined, again citing their social inequality.

That evening, the Mercers' worst fears were confirmed. Word reached them that Sarah was at a house of ill repute at Pine and Twelfth Streets, in a state of mental derangement. The girl was brought back to Queen Street, where she revealed that Heberton had indeed stolen the most valuable and irreplaceable possession of a respectable young woman: her virginity.

Singleton returned home early the next morning, exhausted after searching all night for his sister. Upon learning of Sarah's fate, the normally gentle youth went berserk and threatened to kill her. He was quickly subdued, and his father and brother-in-law left to find Heberton. When they returned empty-handed, Singleton stormed out, determined to hunt down his sister's seducer. He spent the next thirty-six hours searching the city's dives for Heberton, drinking heavily, showing off a loaded pistol and behaving irrationally.

When Heberton learned that Mercer was gunning for him, he sought out James C. Vandyke, a lawyer friend. Heberton remained at Vandyke's home on Walnut Street opposite the State House Yard while the lawyer arranged to spirit him away to a friend's country estate outside Camden. Despite Vandyke's attempts at secrecy, Singleton learned of his enemy's plans and followed him onto the Camden ferry. What Heberton hoped would be a pleasant hunting trip in the Jersey wetlands turned into his appointment with death on Friday, February 10, 1843.

After the panic died down aboard the *John Fitch*, Mercer was placed in the carriage driver's charge, while Vandyke tried to comfort his dying friend. The carriage was directed to nearby Cake's Hotel. There, according to the *Inquirer*, "Mr. Heberton was carried into the waiting room, when, being laid on the carpet, he gave one gasp and expired." Singleton Mercer was taken into custody by the Camden sheriff.

The following morning, an inquest was held at Cake's Hotel. Five doctors examined Heberton's body and determined that he had been killed by the first of Mercer's four shots. The bullet had entered his upper back, shattering the left shoulder blade and a rib before tearing through the lungs and lodging in his heart. While undressing the corpse, the physicians discovered that Heberton had been carrying a pistol and a spring-blade knife. The inquest jury returned a verdict of "willful murder against S. Mercer," who was conveyed to the jail at Woodbury, the Gloucester County seat (Camden County would not be incorporated until 1844).

As news of the murder reached Philadelphia, journalists from the city's twelve daily and weekly newspapers descended on Woodbury. They were joined by reporters from New York, Baltimore and elsewhere, who transformed the remote village into a media circus. Well before the trial began, many reporters had condemned Heberton and exonerated Mercer. "What a lesson to the seducer!" huffed the *Public Ledger*. The *North American* noted that "the sympathy of the community is with Mercer," since "any father, any brother, any man who merits the name of man will confess that if human nature might in any case ask an excuse for the willful shedding of blood, this case must come within the rule." Only the *Inquirer*, which catered to a wealthier readership, did not rush to judgment against Heberton.

Many reporters cast the scandal as a modern-day morality play, with a distinctly democratic slant. On the side of good, there were the Mercers: gray-haired father Thomas, an industrious Irish (but Protestant) immigrant who had achieved the American dream; Eliza, his loyal and uncomplaining wife; his son Singleton, who labored diligently as a bookkeeper at a cotton brokerage; and his precious daughter Sarah, a product of Sunday schools and ladies' academies.

On the side of evil, there was Mahlon Hutchinson Heberton, that thrice-named, slothful symbol of Old Philadelphia's entitled aristocracy. Like Varney, the penny-dreadful vampire of the period, Heberton devoured innocence and destroyed the lives of decent, productive citizens like the Mercers. To enhance the melodrama, reporters exaggerated the socioeconomic gap between the two families, even though the Mercers were probably wealthier than the Hebertons. Some accounts mistakenly described Thomas Mercer as a former mechanic rather than as an affluent retired merchant with significant real estate holdings.

On February 14—St. Valentine's Day—Mahlon Hutchinson Heberton was buried. Nearly two thousand people, many of them young women, watched the meager cortège of three carriages and a hearse proceed from the Heberton residence at Ninth and Arch to the Central Presbyterian Church at Eighth and Cherry. Mrs. Heberton walked the funeral route, supported by two friends. The *North American* used the occasion to preach yet another sermon:

> *The spectacle was a melancholy one, and full of warning to those who, in the pursuit of pleasure, forget the commandments of God, the dictates of conscience, the rights of individuals, and the peace, purity, and laws of society.*

The trial of Singleton Mercer for the "deliberate, intentional, and premeditated killing" of Mahlon H. Heberton began on March 28, 1843, in the Woodbury Courthouse. The prosecution was led by George P. Mollison, attorney general for the State of New Jersey, and Thomas D. Carpenter, prosecuting attorney for Gloucester County. Thanks to his father's fortune, Mercer was defended by seven of Philadelphia's finest lawyers, including former New Jersey governor Peter D. Vroom and Peter A. Browne, later the solicitor for Philadelphia County.

The defense attorneys did not dispute that Singleton Mercer had killed Heberton in cold blood. But, they argued, Mercer had been driven momentarily mad by the shock of having his beloved sister seduced by Heberton, with no legal recourse. The temporary insanity defense was not new. In 1838, Peter A. Browne had employed it successfully to defend a Philadelphia confectioner named Wood who had killed his daughter after she married against his will.

In his opening arguments for the defense, attorney Browne listed the numerous ailments that predisposed Mercer to madness: "He is…of fragile form and bilious, he is afflicted with dreadful constipation, and at the age of twelve years was severely attacked with the croup—all tending to produce derangement of the intellect." Once Mercer learned of his sister's ruin, Browne told the jury, his "reason was gone—it was too much for his weak frame. He roamed through the streets—and every man and woman, he believed, cried 'Kill him, kill him!'"

The defense also attempted to save Singleton from the noose by condemning his victim. "And what shall I say of Mahlon Hutchinson Heberton?" Browne asked rhetorically.

> *I have no desire to wound the feelings of his family and highly respectable connexions. But Heberton was an abandoned libertine, in profession and in practice. He followed no business—his companions were libertines and the only commerce he followed was* seduction!

For two days, witnesses described Mercer's erratic behavior from the moment of Sarah's disappearance, when the pious youth suddenly became a foul-mouthed, hard-drinking hysteric. Lawyers battled over the legal definition of insanity, or "monomania," and whether Mercer's conduct fit the description or was just clever acting.

On the third day of the trial, Thursday, March 30, the defense produced its star witness: Sarah Gardner Mercer. Aware of the emotional impact that the young girl's testimony would produce, the prosecution objected strenuously, arguing that Heberton was not on trial. Disingenuously, the defense explained that it did not offer this testimony "because Heberton was a libertine—an enemy of mankind" but because it wished to show "the provocation for the act of Singleton Mercer, and its justification." The judge allowed the witness.

Even before she uttered one word, Sarah Mercer created a sensation. Peter A. Browne left the courtroom to fetch her but came back to announce that there would be a delay because Sarah was suffering convulsions. He left again and returned with Sarah leaning heavily on his arm, accompanied by her mother, older sister and other female friends. Sarah entered the courtroom sobbing and moaning and needed several minutes to calm down once she was seated.

Sarah told the jury that she had met Heberton by accident in early January, shortly before her sixteenth birthday, while shopping with a friend on Chestnut Street. Passing by Heberton and another man, Sarah told her friend that she thought Heberton was Mr. Bastido, a Spanish gentleman she had met at a Christmas party. The two men overheard Sarah and seized on the opportunity to flirt with her and her friend. When Sarah went out on an errand the next evening, "Mr. Bastido" was waiting for her. After the two had met for several secret evening strolls, Heberton revealed his true identity.

On their sixth rendezvous, Sarah stammered, she and Heberton stopped at a house in Elizabeth Street, a notorious red-light district. When Heberton said that it was a friend's house and that they should go in and warm up, Sarah refused. But Heberton insisted. A mulatto woman ushered them upstairs to a second-floor bedroom. When Sarah saw the bed, she screamed, but Heberton pulled out a pistol and ordered her to be silent. Sobbing, Sarah related how Heberton removed her bonnet and cloak and then carried her to the bed. While Heberton took off his coat, Sarah tried to escape. Heberton threw her back on the bed and loosened his suspenders and pantaloons. The courtroom was silent as Sarah whispered, "He then violated my person."

Before they left the house, Heberton told Sarah that he loved her and wanted to marry her and take her away to New Orleans. When Sarah refused to meet him again and insisted on telling her parents what he had done, Heberton threatened to spread the word that Sarah herself had picked him up in the street and brought him to the house. For unknown reasons—fear of exposure, hope that Heberton would marry her and save her reputation or perhaps even infatuation—the girl met Heberton several times over the next few weeks at Elizabeth Street and other assignation houses.

Then, in early February, while Sarah was visiting her married older sister, her father's servant girl arrived with the news that Thomas Mercer had learned of her attachment to Heberton and wanted her home immediately. Sarah said the servant told her "that she didn't know what my father would do to me." Terrified, Sarah went to the last place she had met Heberton, a house at Pine and Twelfth. When the landlady was unable to find Heberton for the hysterical girl after two days, she sent a message to the Mercers about their daughter.

Sarah concluded her testimony by saying, "During my walks with Mr. Heberton, he said to me that he liked me better than any young lady he had ever seen." Despite this ambiguous statement, her emotional performance—supported by a Greek chorus of sobbing female relatives in the front row—made a powerful impression. In cross-examination, Sarah rebuffed the prosecution's attempts to call her innocence into question. She had gone upstairs with Heberton at Elizabeth Street because in her home, the parlor was on the second floor. She had not seen the bed until Heberton pushed her into the room and locked the door. Yes, she had met several of Heberton's friends. No, she had never spent time with them or with any other man as she had with Heberton.

The trial continued for five more days, with more witnesses testifying to Singleton's irrational behavior and more legal arguments on the nature of insanity. But after Sarah's testimony, there was little doubt as to its outcome. On Wednesday, April 5, the two sides offered their closing arguments. Prosecuting Attorney Thomas Carpenter took three hours to present the state's case in the morning.

After lunch, Governor Peter Vroom concluded for the defense in a bravura performance that lasted nearly seven hours. "He [Heberton] took her in his arms," Vroom thundered, "laid her down on that altar, and offered her up to the God of his lusts!" He rehashed Sarah's ordeal in graphic detail.

> *Sarah struggled and cried out aloud to the last; but alarmed, almost fainting, intimidated by his threats, and injured by his violence, she was at length overpowered—when in the most brutal and violent manner he VIOLATED her PERSON—committed a RAPE upon her.*

On Thursday, April 6, the judge gave detailed instructions to the jury for eight hours, from 9:00 a.m. until 5:00 p.m. The jury retired and, after only half an hour, announced that it had reached a verdict. Spectators stampeded back from nearby taverns, leaving their dinners half-eaten. The entire courtroom held its breath as the foreman rose and announced the verdict.

Not guilty.

The room exploded in an uproar of delight, despite cries of "Silence!" and "Order!" from the constable. Singleton and Thomas Mercer were nearly smothered by joyful supporters. When the verdict was announced outdoors, the cheering lasted for fifteen minutes. Singleton Mercer was taken back to jail—not as a prisoner but to wait until the commotion had subsided. Journalists rushed to the waterfront, hiring rowboats and sloops to ferry them back to Philadelphia with their hot story.

Not everyone was elated by Mercer's acquittal. Isaac Mickle, editor of the *Camden Eagle* and a lawyer himself, wrote in his journal that "Mercer, the murderer, has been acquitted by the leather-headed jackasses who were picked to try him. Jerseymen can say nothing hereafter about Pennsylvania justice."

Singleton and Thomas Mercer returned quietly to Philadelphia the following morning, crossing the Delaware River at Gloucester Point and arriving via Point House Road, south of the city. A large crowd had gathered at Walnut Street Wharf, expecting them to arrive there. Instead, they greeted Mercer's lawyers, who marched up Walnut Street in triumph, tipping their hats to the cheering throng.

Newspapers across the country hailed Singleton Mercer as a protector of feminine virtue. The citizens of Louisville, Kentucky, announced plans to present him with a gold medal. More thoughtful commentators urged the passage of stricter laws to prosecute seducers and rapists, preventing future "Mercer tragedies." Singleton appeared anxious to move on, opening his own cotton brokerage business on South Front Street. But Isaac Mickle, never a great fan, reported in May that "Mercer, the assassin" was spending much time in Woodbury and had gotten "into a scrape with some of the girls."

The "Mercer tragedy" was about to take on a new and more lurid existence. George Lippard, a Germantown-born novelist and journalist, covered the Mercer trial for a Philadelphia penny paper called the *Citizen Soldier*. In the fall of 1844, Lippard began to publish a weekly serialized novel called *The Quaker City, or the Monks of Monk Hall*. The sprawling novel blended supernaturalism, gore, social satire, political protest and mild pornography to create a grotesque portrait of a Philadelphia that was "without all purity, within all rottenness and dead men's bones." The fictional Monk Hall of the title was a labyrinthine structure in Southwark where the city's most respectable men by day assembled at night for unspeakable acts of debauchery, rape and sadism.

Mary Arlington, Byrnewood
Arlington and Gustavus Lorrimer
in George Lippard's *The Quaker City*.
These characters were based on
Sarah Mercer, Singleton Mercer
and Mahlon Heberton.

The main plot of *The Quaker City* was drawn directly from the Mercer-Heberton case, with Gustavus Lorrimer standing in for Heberton, Byrnewood Arlington for Singleton and Mary Arlington for Sarah. In the novel, Gus Lorrimer and Byrnewood Arlington are friends who delight in ruining virtuous women (a secondary plot describes Byrnewood's seduction and abandonment of a servant girl, a charge leveled at Mercer during his trial). Lippard's physical description of the two characters mirrors their real-life counterparts, with "tall, manly and muscular" Lorrimer holding sway over "slight yet well-proportioned" Arlington.

Byrnewood gleefully assists Lorrimer's plans to seduce an innocent young girl at Monk Hall, only to discover too late that Lorrimer's prey is his own sister, Mary. In the book's climax, Lorrimer is trapped on a boat crossing the icy Delaware on Christmas morning with Byrnewood. The vengeful brother shoots and kills Lorrimer, then hysterically calls for music so he can dance over the corpse. An epilogue shows Mary Arlington living with her brother far from civilization, still hopelessly and rather insanely in love with her dead despoiler.

Despite mixed reviews, *The Quaker City* was an unparalleled popular success from its first installment. Each week, the newspaper carrying the serial was snapped up by Philadelphians, who speculated on the real-life models for its characters. When the complete story was published in May 1845, it sold over sixty thousand copies in its first year, making it the bestselling book America had ever seen. Lippard grew wealthy and used his profits to found his own newspaper entitled—what else?—the *Quaker City*.

Singleton Mercer's reaction to the serialized novel is unknown. But when Lippard attempted to mount a dramatic version of *The Quaker City* at the Chestnut Street Theatre in November 1844, Mercer expressed his displeasure in no uncertain terms. As a crowd watched, he defaced a playbill outside the theatre and then requested two hundred tickets "for the purpose of a grand row." Philadelphia had been through a series of deadly anti-Catholic riots earlier that year, and its politicians dreaded an equally bloody theatre riot. Upon the advice of the mayor, the theatre manager postponed, and then canceled, *The Quaker City*.

After that, Singleton Mercer vanished into obscurity for nearly a decade. In December 1852, an item appeared about an early Christmas morning brawl in an oyster cellar at Third and Chestnut Streets, during which Mercer was seriously injured. According to the newspaper, "Mercer stated that he had been shot; but it was evident upon examination of his person that he had been struck upon the head by a stick, and pretty extensively 'shot in the neck.'" In other words, he was stinking drunk.

The Christmas brawl may have served as an epiphany for the drifting Mercer. In the summer of 1855, the cities of Norfolk and Portsmouth, Virginia, were devastated by a yellow fever epidemic that killed more than 10 percent of their combined populations. Remembering their own struggles with yellow fever, Philadelphians assisted the plague-ridden cities by dispatching money, food and volunteer doctors and nurses.

Mercer, then thirty-five, volunteered as a nurse on August 22, insisting that "it was a duty which man owed to his fellow-man to assist in the time of pestilence." He was sent to Portsmouth, where he promptly contracted yellow fever himself. The hapless Mercer died on September 9, less than three weeks after his arrival. Reporting on his death, the *Richmond Daily Dispatch* described Mercer as a "man of generous impulses, whose life is another sacrifice to humanity."

Mercer was interred in a temporary grave, along with ten other doctors, nurses and druggists from Philadelphia who had died from the fever. They remained there for over three years, while their native city raised funds to erect a fitting memorial. In early 1859, the eleven bodies were disinterred and shipped back to Philadelphia. On January 18, the remains of the nine male yellow fever victims were placed in an underground vault at Laurel Hill Cemetery (with Victorian propriety, the two female victims were buried

Above, left: The Yellow Fever Victims' Monument at Laurel Hill Cemetery, erected in 1859. Singleton Mercer lies here with eight other volunteers to fever-stricken Portsmouth, Virginia.

Above, right: The Heberton family monument, moved to Laurel Hill Cemetery in 1848 from the Central Presbyterian Church on Cherry Street. *Photograph by Lawrence M. Arrigale.*

separately). Above the vault rose a twenty-five-foot-tall marble column atop a square base engraved with scenes of charity and sacrifice.

Singleton Mercer still lies beneath the Yellow Fever Monument at the northern edge of Laurel Hill Cemetery, overlooking the Schuylkill River. South of his memorial, a smaller monument marks the grave of Mahlon Hutchinson Heberton and his parents. Their remains were relocated to Laurel Hill when the Central Presbyterian Church sold its Cherry Street churchyard in 1848. Today, only a short walk separates the final resting places of two young men whose lives were disrupted forever aboard the Camden ferry on an icy night in 1843.

And what of Sarah Mercer, the young woman whose innocent confusion of a stranger for a family friend triggered the avalanche of rape, murder and despair? Pending further research, her fate is unknown. Did she change her name and move away from Philadelphia? Did she face down her disgrace, marry and have children? Or did she retreat to a relative's attic and become the eccentric maiden aunt whom everyone pitied for unspoken reasons? Did she ever visit her brother's tomb at Laurel Hill? If so, did she stroll south to stand before Mahlon Heberton's grave, to curse him to hell, to forgive him or to wonder if he had, indeed, liked her better than any young lady he had ever seen?

"IS THERE NO LAW TO HANG THEM?"

Body Snatching at Lebanon Cemetery, 1882

> *Grave*, n. *A place in which the dead are laid to await the coming of the medical student.*
> —*Ambrose Bierce*, The Devil's Dictionary

December 4, 1882. The four men shivered in the cold night air, despite being huddled together in a small carriage hidden in the darkness on Passyunk Avenue near Eighteenth Street in South Philadelphia. Across from their cab, on the north side of Passyunk, the marble tombstones of Lebanon Cemetery glowed in the moonlight. Passing a flask filled with liquid warmth, the men studied the graveyard, as if waiting for spirits to rise from the irregular rows of graves that staggered across the winter-withered lawn.

Lebanon was one of Philadelphia's two private burial grounds for African Americans, who were barred from nearly all of the city's white-owned rural cemeteries. At its founding in 1849, Lebanon had been truly rural, the wooden spire of its Gothic chapel soaring above the open fields of Passyunk Township. Now the graveyard was hemmed in by the row houses and factories of fast-growing South Philadelphia. Its five and a half acres were packed with nearly seventeen thousand corpses, or over three thousand bodies per acre. Overcrowded and decrepit, Lebanon was a grim illustration of the lack of options available to African Americans who wished a dignified burial in segregated Philadelphia.

The four men shivered as they waited for their signal to act. They jumped, startled, at a knock on the carriage door. A strongly built man with a thick beard and mustache opened the door.

"They're coming," he whispered.

The four men slipped out of the carriage. From within the cemetery, faint noises gradually grew louder: the rhythmic thud of a horse's hooves and the rattle of wagon wheels bouncing along a dirt road. Suddenly, a shape emerged from the darkness—a one-horse wagon, trundling toward the main gate.

"Get ready." Their leader pulled a revolver from his pocket as the wagon turned east on Passyunk Avenue.

"Now!" the bearded man hissed. He rushed into the road and halted the wagon, pointing his pistol at the driver. His four companions followed him, aiming their guns at the two passengers.

"What the hell do you want?" cursed the driver. "We haven't any money!"

"Are you Frank McNamee?" the bearded man demanded.

"Who wants to know?"

"Louis Megargee of the *Press*. I have a warrant for your arrest on charges of grave robbing, McNamee. Get down from the wagon."

Louis Megargee and his fellow reporters confront the grave robbers outside Lebanon Cemetery on December 4, 1882, as depicted by *Frank Leslie's Illustrated Newspaper*.

Slowly, the three men—two white and one black—climbed to the ground, raising their hands. Megargee lit a lantern and jumped into the wagon, throwing back the tarpaulin that concealed its contents. He gulped involuntarily as he stared at the nauseating cargo he had only seen at a distance until then. In the glow of the lantern, he could make out six naked bodies piled like firewood on the wagon floor. The four men and two women were of various ages, but all were stiff with rigor mortis and reeked of dirt and decay. These six African Americans had been cheated out of a decent burial to be taken to Jefferson Medical College and dissected by white medical students.

Louis Megargee, city editor of the *Philadelphia Press*, had finally broken the story he had been working on all year. While writing a feature on medical schools, Megargee had noticed that Jefferson Medical College seemed to enjoy an endless supply of corpses for dissection in its anatomy classes. A medical school's survival depended on providing its students with bodies for training in anatomy, the most prestigious and popular discipline. In Philadelphia, there were usually only four hundred bodies available per year for more than one thousand medical students. Jefferson should have been fighting with its rival schools over the limited number of unclaimed corpses from the general hospital, almshouse and morgue. Yet its students were always well supplied with specimens, nearly all of them African American.

Megargee spent many nights in the spring of 1882 hidden in the shadows of the Jefferson Medical School hospital, a gloomy Gothic pile at Tenth and Sansom Streets. He realized that Jefferson was regularly receiving African American corpses from the same team of men, who always drove their one-horse wagon into the hospital courtyard in the small hours of the morning. Megargee discovered the men's identities and tracked their midnight trips to and from Lebanon Cemetery. But before he could expose the grave robbers, the school term ended and the deliveries stopped.

Megargee had to wait until late November before the men resumed their trips. On the evening of December 4, 1882, the journalist hid in the cemetery and watched Frank McNamee and his helpers load their wagon. He then alerted his colleagues from the *Press* to help him capture the body snatchers. The fact that it fell to five reporters to equip themselves with pistols and an arrest warrant to collar the body snatchers illustrates the relaxed attitude of Philadelphia police toward this kind of crime, especially when African Americans were the victims.

McNamee was taken to the Central Police Station at Fifth and Chestnut with his accomplices—Levi Chew, a black groundskeeper at Lebanon, and

Henry "Dutch" Pillet, a one-eyed white man. Soon the police brought in Levi's brother Robert, superintendent at Lebanon Cemetery since 1871.

Early on the morning of December 5, a hearing was held for the four conspirators in which the full extent of the horror was exposed. Graves had been plundered at Lebanon Cemetery for over nine years, with the full cooperation of Superintendent Chew. Several hundred corpses had been sold illegally to Jefferson Medical College for dissection during that time. When demand was especially strong, the grave robbers did not even wait to dig up bodies. They opened the coffins of the newly dead in the receiving vault, snatched the corpse and buried a weighted coffin before the grieving family the next day.

McNamee, who ran a normal delivery service during daylight hours, told police he had taken over the body snatching business from his brother-in-law, who had moved to Maryland three years earlier. McNamee surrendered two keys to the rooms at Jefferson where bodies were prepared for dissection. He refused to divulge who at the school had given him the keys or accepted the bodies. He did disclose that Jefferson paid eight dollars for each body, of which three dollars went to Robert Chew, the supplier, and one dollar to McNamee, the delivery man. The remaining four dollars were split between Levi Chew and Henry Pillet, who dug up the bodies. (Robert Chew told police that he preferred not to handle the dead, since he believed in ghosts.)

As word of the desecration spread through Philadelphia's African American community, a mob gathered at the courthouse, demanding that the four ghouls be turned over for lynching. After the judge committed McNamee, Pillet and the Chews to jail in default of $5,000 bail, the grave robbers were attacked by the waiting crowd when they left the courtroom. Eleven policemen beat back the enraged spectators with clubs as they escorted the prisoners to jail.

Hundreds of other African Americans gathered at the city morgue at Noble and Beach Streets, desperate to know if their relatives were among the six bodies. One man screamed when he found his twenty-nine-year-old brother. An elderly woman wailed that she had begged at the wharves where her husband once worked to collect twenty-two dollars for his burial. Now he, too, was among the desecrated corpses. Other families who had lost family members felt little relief at not finding them at the morgue. Instead, they raced to Lebanon, terrified that their loved ones had already been removed. Under pressure from the black community, the Health Office issued thirteen permits to open graves at the cemetery.

To learn that a relative's body has been stolen and hacked apart is a devastating experience for anyone. But for nineteenth-century African Americans, whose lives were constricted on every side by discrimination, it was a particularly loathsome fate. A proper funeral with coffin, tombstone and cemetery plot was their last opportunity to obtain the dignity denied them in life. "Going to the colleges"—having one's body dissected at a medical school along with the city's paupers, drunks and whores—was an admission that one had died without a shred of comfort or respect. To have struggled to bury a loved one properly and then to discover that he had still ended up on a dissecting slab became the ultimate obscenity.

On December 7, Philadelphia's African American community held an "indignation meeting" at Liberty Hall on Lombard Street. Tearful and angry blacks accused Lebanon Cemetery's board of trustees of complicity in the illegal grave robbing. The day before, journalist H. Price Williams had gotten into a fistfight with Guy M. Burton, president of the cemetery board and a prominent undertaker, at an opened grave at Lebanon. Now Williams attacked Burton verbally, saying that he and the rest of the trustees should be behind bars.

Lebanon's trustees immediately launched their spin control. Later that day, Guy M. Burton gave a private interview in his home at 616 Pine Street to a reporter for the *Inquirer*, who described Burton as "a stout, fine-looking colored man, of considerable intelligence, prominent in the colored political organizations in this city." Burton swore that the trustees were ignorant of the activities of Robert Chew, who had already been fired and whose family had been forced to vacate the superintendent's cottage. Mollified, the reporter concluded that the attacks on Burton were prompted by "the envy and jealousy of some who have not risen to prominence in the colored community."

Simultaneously, the Health Office—perhaps with prompting from the cemetery trustees—declared that no more permits would be granted to open graves at Lebanon. Their decision was "a sanitary precaution, owing to the fact that several bodies taken up already are those who died from small pox, diphtheria, and other infectious ailments." This decision meant that many African Americans would never know the fate of their relatives. Meanwhile, Mayor Samuel George King dismissed demands for guards at Lebanon, saying that he didn't have the men available.

On December 13, Frank McNamee, Henry Pillet, Levi Chew and Robert Chew were indicted on six charges by the grand jury, with their trial scheduled to begin the next day. Deciding that he had nothing left to lose, McNamee fingered Dr. William S. Forbes, demonstrator of anatomy at Jefferson Medical College, as "the instigator and supporter of the nefarious plot." In an interview with the *Philadelphia Press* that was carried by newspapers across the country, McNamee insisted that Forbes himself had paid for bodies he knew had been taken from Lebanon illegally and had given McNamee the keys to Jefferson's dissecting rooms.

McNamee told the *Press* that he had visited Forbes's home to express his concern over the legality of his actions. According to McNamee, the doctor had assured him that he would not get into trouble, saying, "Do you suppose the gentlemen connected with our faculty would let you go ahead if you were doing wrong? Why, Judges Allison and Ludlow are on our Board of Trustees, and do you suppose they would permit this thing if it were wrong?" McNamee noted that Forbes had even given him a raise, "considering that I had to go so far downtown at a late hour at night and in all kinds of weather."

McNamee's accusations sent shock waves through Philadelphia's interconnected medical and social elites. William S. Forbes was one of the city's most distinguished physicians and academics. An 1852 graduate of Jefferson, he had served as a surgeon in both the Crimean and Civil Wars before opening a private school of anatomy and surgery in Philadelphia in 1870. In 1879, he had returned to his alma mater as demonstrator of anatomy, in addition to serving as senior surgeon at Episcopal Hospital. Forbes quickly became Jefferson's star attraction, respected by his colleagues and worshipped by his students. Tall, handsome and charming, he was also wealthy and well connected. His wife, Celenaire, was the only surviving child of the founder of the American Life Insurance Company.

Ironically, the alleged instigator of the Lebanon horror was the author of the Pennsylvania Anatomy Act of 1867, the first law to provide medical schools in Philadelphia and Pittsburgh with unclaimed cadavers for dissection. By establishing a legal mechanism for the appropriation of unclaimed corpses to medical schools, the "Ghastly Act" was meant to improve medical training, reduce malpractice and end illegal trafficking in human bodies.

The act was also designed to clean up the reputation of Philadelphia physicians, whose body snatching had been one of the city's dirty little secrets since it emerged as America's medical capital in colonial days. All of the great eighteenth-century surgeons, including William Shippen and Philip Syng Physick, had been accused of "resurrectionism." Shippen, when attacked by a mob for his activities, protested that he had taken bodies from the potter's field but had never touched one from a proper churchyard.

Conditions worsened in the early nineteenth century, when the superintendent of the public cemetery had grown rich on bribes from medical schools to ensure their allotment of paupers' cadavers during "dissecting season." Newspapers regularly printed accounts of Philadelphia doctors and students digging up their own bodies and battling over choice specimens.

But as the medical profession grew more professional after the Civil War, it wished to wash its hands of the stink of the grave. While bodies were still snatched in Philadelphia, they were snatched by lower-class middlemen who delivered them discreetly to doctor's assistants late at night, with no questions asked. If a prominent figure like Forbes were to be convicted of grave robbing, it would be a major setback for all American physicians.

Despite these concerns, pressure from the African American community forced Philadelphia's district attorney to act. In mid-December, an arrest warrant was issued for Forbes on charges of conspiring with McNamee and others to despoil graves at Lebanon Cemetery and to violate the right of sepulture by disinterring bodies. Forbes was released after his attorney paid his $5,000 bail.

Meanwhile, trial began for McNamee, Pillet and the two Chews, all of whom had been languishing in prison, unable to post their bail. A jury was selected, consisting of eleven whites and one black, Charles H. Davis, who was named foreman. When the jury heard the charges against the four men, Davis was heard to mutter, "Is there no law to hang them?" All four were found guilty, but their sentencing was postponed until after Forbes was brought to trial. Since Frank McNamee was sure to be used as a witness against Forbes, this raises the question of whether his sentence was to depend on the testimony he provided in the later trial.

William S. Forbes's trial did not begin until March 12, 1883. Arguing for the prosecution, the district attorney stated that if Forbes had known that the bodies brought by McNamee were obtained illegally, then he was as guilty as if he had dug them up with his own hands. The prosecution then presented its star witness, Frank McNamee, who told the same story he had told the *Press* in December: Forbes himself had accepted and paid for many bodies that he knew were obtained illegally from Lebanon; he had given McNamee keys to Jefferson; and when McNamee had expressed his concerns to Forbes, the physician had reassured him and asked him to continue.

Forbes's attorney, Richard P. White, promptly demolished what little credibility McNamee possessed, pointing out that the grave robber had once spent two years in jail for robbing a liquor store. White also charged that after

McNamee's arrest in December, the accused had sent his wife to see Forbes and demand that the physician post bail for him. When Forbes refused, McNamee had "exposed" the doctor in the *Press*. White also produced Jefferson employees who swore that they alone had accepted bodies from McNamee, who had represented them as having been legally obtained.

William S. Forbes then took the stand in his own defense. A riveting lecturer in the classroom, he proved equally commanding in the courtroom, testifying that in twenty-five years of teaching anatomy he had never received a single body he had known to be either buried or claimed. Although he knew McNamee slightly as a provider of bodies, Forbes swore that he had never spoken to him about how the bodies were obtained. He had neither accepted bodies from McNamee nor paid him. That was handled by his assistants. Forbes even denied entering the room at Jefferson where corpses were received or seeing them until they were on the dissecting table, injected and embalmed.

When Forbes was asked if he had ever wondered about McNamee's endless supply of African American corpses, he adopted a "don't ask, don't tell" attitude: "In the great desire to teach surgery and anatomy, it would not do to inquire where every body came from. If that was done, Philadelphia would not be a great metropolis of scientific teaching."

After Forbes's testimony, a veritable who's who of prominent Philadelphians vouched for his character: financier Anthony J. Drexel, former mayor Daniel Fox, attorney C. Stuart Patterson, General Lucius H. Warren, trolley magnate George Fairman and Judge Craig Biddle. Dr. D. Hayes Agnew, the University of Pennsylvania professor of surgery who would later be immortalized by Thomas Eakins, testified that "it was not usual for a demonstrator of anatomy in the best colleges…to inquire or trace the source from where the separate bodies came."

Two days later, on March 17, 1883, the jury declared Forbes not guilty on all charges in the Lebanon Cemetery case. The courtroom erupted in applause. Most Philadelphia papers—except for Louis Megargee's persnickety *Press*—also cheered Forbes's acquittal. The *Inquirer* gushed that there was "gratification at the result of the trial, mingled, however, with regret that an innocent man should have been unavoidably subjected to so severe an ordeal."

When William S. Forbes entered his lecture hall on Monday, March 19, he received a thunderous ovation from all 569 students of the Jefferson Medical College. He was presented with a gigantic flower basket, "so large that it looked like a moving garden bed of blooms and foliage," topped by a crown of red, white and yellow roses. The *Inquirer* reporter sighed that "the pleasure of looking at [the bouquet] was mingled with regret that anything so beautiful should ever fade." The honor of Philadelphia's medical community had been upheld, with lots of lovely blossoms to blot out the stench of rotting flesh.

On March 29, the Philadelphia Quarter Sessions Court tied up the loose strings of the tawdry affair by sentencing the four original conspirators. The African American Chew brothers received the longest sentences: former superintendent Robert was given two years in prison, while Levi received eighteen months. Frank McNamee was sentenced to eight months, and Henry Pillet to four. All of the sentences were from the committal date of December 15, 1882, which meant that McNamee would be free in four months and Pillet in two weeks.

The judge explained the difference in his sentencing of the black and white men by noting that Robert Chew had violated his position of trust as superintendent of the cemetery. His brother Levi, another cemetery worker, had also betrayed his employers' trust, although to a lesser extent. But Frank McNamee and Henry Pillet, "as strangers in their relations to the cemetery company, have been guilty of no breach of trust, and Pillet, having no part in the planning of this crime, [was] the least guilty of all." So even though Levi Chew and Henry Pillet dug up the same bodies, Chew's groundskeeper job at Lebanon earned him an additional fourteen months in jail.

Forbes rebounded quickly after his vindication. Thanks to his lobbying efforts, the Pennsylvania legislature soon passed a new anatomy law that required officials at every state institution (including prisons, morgues, hospitals and poorhouses) to give medical schools the bodies of their dead inmates, unless claimed by relatives. This new law not only provided anatomists with a reliable supply of bodies, but it also reduced the taxpayers' bill for the burial of unclaimed corpses. Additionally, the law overturned a provision from the 1867 act that allowed the poor to avoid dissection by requesting burial at the state's expense before their death.

When William S. Forbes died in 1905, he was perhaps Philadelphia's most revered and respected physician. Since 1886, he had held the position of anatomy and clinical surgery at Jefferson Medical College, which had become one of the leading medical schools in America. Forbes's front-page obituary in the *Inquirer* enumerated the doctor's many honors, memberships, publications, inventions and innovations.

William S. Forbes, the physician who had no idea where the bodies for his anatomy classes came from. *Archives and Special Collections, Thomas Jefferson University.*

But Forbes's crowning accomplishment, according to the obituary, was

> *his authorship of the original Anatomy act of Pennsylvania in 1863* [sic]
> *and its amendment in 1883. This act has placed the procuring of subjects*
> *for dissection in the various medical schools in Pennsylvania upon a legal*
> *basis, and has been the greatest aid in the advancement of medical science.*

Thomas Eakins's full-length portrait of Forbes, commissioned by Jefferson students in the year of his death (and recently sold by the school), shows the elderly physician with his hand resting on a parchment document labeled "The Anatomy Act."

Despite the scandal, Lebanon Cemetery would survive almost as long as Dr. Forbes. Growing more crowded and decrepit every year, it continued to illustrate how desperately limited African Americans' burial options were in Philadelphia. In 1898, the Board of Health condemned Lebanon as a health hazard. Five years later, the city acquired the cemetery for $90,000, ostensibly to straighten the intersection of Passyunk Avenue and Nineteenth Street. At that time, most of the bodies were removed to Eden, a newly founded rural cemetery for African Americans in Delaware County.

The same year that Lebanon closed, Jefferson Medical College demolished its old buildings at Tenth and Sansom for an addition to its hospital. An *Inquirer* article dated July 22, 1903, describes the discovery of cavernous underground vaults, accessible via a ceiling trapdoor that communicated with the dissecting rooms above. Human bones were uncovered in the vaults—not surprising since they "were used formerly to hide the bodies required for dissection, the majority of them having been stolen from graveyards." With a fine disregard for accuracy, the reporter continued:

> *The "snatching" of the body of a negro from the old Lebanon Cemetery, at Nineteenth street and Passyunk avenue in 1880, led to an investigation and exposure, which resulted in the establishment by the Legislature of the State Anatomical Board, which did away forever with the practice of body snatching.*

Despite the *Inquirer*'s confident statement, body snatching and the abuse of the dead are very much with us today. In 2008, three Philadelphia morticians pled guilty to participating in a body-snatching ring that illegally harvested parts from hundreds of corpses—including the cadavers of cancer, HIV or hepatitis C victims—for surgical use, without notifying either the corpses' relatives or the recipients of the body parts.

Given the long and continuing saga of body snatching in Philadelphia, it's hardly surprising that our city became one of the early centers of cremation in America.

THE BEST LITTLE WHOREHOUSE IN PHILLY

James R. Applegate's Flying Circus, 1890

Round the world in 80 days,
Once great, now nothing in it,
Since Applegate, Franklin and Vine
Makes 80 trips a minute.
—ad for Applegate's Palace of Flying Animals, December 21, 1890

In 1890, the elders of the First Moravian Church of Philadelphia faced a quandary. When their church had been built at the southwest corner of Franklin and Wood Streets in 1856, it stood in a quiet residential neighborhood. Thirty-four years later, it was smack in the middle of the city's most notorious red-light district, the area north of Franklin Square known as the Tenderloin. The house of God was encircled by saloons, dance halls, burlesque theatres and brothels. Families coming to Sunday worship had to sidestep the sprawled bodies of drunks sleeping off Saturday night's spree.

Two years earlier, the elders had put the First Moravian property on the market. They had hoped to realize $60,000 on the sale of the church building and the adjacent lot, which had held their burial ground before its removal to Ivy Hill Cemetery in 1885. The sale would allow them to build a new church at Seventeenth Street and Fairmount Avenue, a more respectable neighborhood. But the highest bid was well below their asking price.

Now James R. Applegate, one of the city's leading photographers, had offered $50,000 for the property. Although this was still less than the elders'

The First Moravian Church at Franklin and Wood Streets, as it appeared when James R. Applegate opened his Palace next door on its former churchyard.

asking price, Applegate would let them remain in the church for at least a year, giving them time to raise additional capital. Combining the talents of Louis Daguerre with those of P.T. Barnum, Applegate planned to erect a large indoor carousel on the former burial ground. He promised that the merry-go-round would not operate on Sunday, allowing the Moravians to worship in peace. For some of the elders, Applegate's offer seemed like manna from heaven. But other vestrymen had doubts about their supposed savior.

Starting in 1860, James R. Applegate had produced some of the first tintypes in Philadelphia. Now the sixty-eight-year-old photographer was a millionaire, thanks to his gigantic Vine Street Galleries, which stretched along the south side of Vine between Eighth and Winter Streets. Before the introduction of the Brownie camera in 1900, most people had their portraits taken at a studio like Applegate's, stiffly posed next to a potted palm before a painted backdrop. Every day in Applegate's emporium, an assembly line of photographers snapped over eight hundred customers, whose pictures were then developed, encased and sold by a bevy of pretty young female assistants. Between his Philadelphia and Atlantic City studios, Applegate was rumored to take in over $50,000 a year.

In 1884, Applegate had expanded into the entertainment business by opening one of the first amusement piers on the Atlantic City Boardwalk, at the foot of Tennessee Avenue. Applegate's Pier extended 625 feet over the ocean and held over ten thousand people at one time in a gargantuan, multitiered structure. Among the pier's attractions was a "Palace of Flying Animals"—an exotic name for a carousel.

The elders of the First Moravian Church were especially divided over Applegate's Pier, which freely mixed the sacred and the profane. His supporters pointed out that Applegate held a concert of sacred music every Sunday night. His detractors argued that on the other six days of the week, pier patrons indulged in salacious new dances like the two-step, watched vulgar vaudeville and even retreated to a "Lover's Pavilion" for kissing and petting.

In October 1890, the pro-Applegate faction won, assisted by the congregation's fervent desire to escape the Tenderloin. Soon, a barnlike wooden structure rose on the old burial ground next to the church, at the northwest corner of Vine and Franklin Streets. Applegate sold his Atlantic City amusement pier and moved its giant carousel to Philadelphia. In early December, newspaper advertisements began to appear:

The New Carousel Opens Tuesday Night Next.
Finest in the World.
A Palace of Flying Animals.
A Paradise for the Children.

The ads promised family-friendly delights like a gigantic pipe organ, free parking for baby carriages, trained nurses to watch the infants while parents frolicked and free boxes of candy for the kiddies. When Applegate's Palace of Flying Animals—also known as Applegate's Merry-Go-Round, Carousel or Flying Circus—opened on December 23, 1890, the line of children and parents stretched around the block.

However wholesome Applegate's Palace was during the day, church members soon realized that it attracted a very different clientele at night. The *American Journal of Photography* described the Palace in cautious terms as being "quite a feature with a certain class of the community, who nightly congregate there to whirl around to the music of a $500 steam organ while viewing themselves in the mirrors on the wall." Others put it more bluntly: the First Moravian Church now stood next door to the biggest, noisiest whorehouse and pick-up joint in Philadelphia. According to one reporter, "Pulpiteers mustered their stirring invective in picturing Applegate's Carrousel…as a place of sin and temptation outrivaling Sodom and Gomorrah."

On the surface, the Palace was just another Tenderloin saloon and dance hall, but on a vaster, more surreal scale. In keeping with the circus theme, all of the employees were costumed as carnival folk. Waitresses wore tights and waiters were dressed as clowns. Bartenders were made up as strong men, their animal-skin outfits revealing brawny arms and chests. Each night, eight of these muscle-bound mixologists served a mob of screaming, drunken customers, lined up two and three deep in front of a one-hundred-foot-long bar.

A canvas canopy, painted in garish colors, hung from the ceiling like a giant circus tent. The dance floor was surrounded by well-padded booths for two, with a wooden carousel animal in front of each booth. Customers had to either climb over or crawl under the animal if they wanted to use the lavatory or take a spin on the carousel in an adjacent chamber. The dimly lit booths offered male patrons sufficient room and privacy for either flirtation or foreplay, depending on the willingness of their companions.

Once these men were ready to proceed further, they didn't have to travel far. More than 150 prostitutes were on the prowl at Applegate's on any given night. About a dozen working girls were on the house payroll, with rooms upstairs. The rest—professionals, part-timers and amateurs—took their johns to nearby boardinghouses or brothels.

Where were the police while all of this debauchery was taking place night after night? Safe inside the Palace, moonlighting as private guards to control the rowdy customers. One plainclothesman stood on the corner outside, directing passersby into the Palace. Another officer shadowed Applegate all night long, making sure that the proprietor was not robbed and that he paid the proper bribes after the 5:00 a.m. closing.

Thanks to his generous payoffs to police and politicians, Applegate was able to operate his circus of sin with impunity. In 1891, he sued William Y. Leader, publisher of the *Sunday Dispatch*, for printing an article that described the Palace as "a rendezvous for professional mashers and loungers and a stamping ground for street-walkers." Applegate won the suit after "Special [police] officer Shyatt, who is detailed at the Palace for special duty…testified as to the good order preserved in the place."

But the city's reformers, led by department store magnate John Wanamaker and *North American* publisher Clayton McMichael, refused to back down. They pressured Mayor Edwin S. Stuart and the City Councils to close Applegate's Palace and other notorious houses of ill repute in the Tenderloin. On Wednesday, January 28, 1892, the largest police raid in Philadelphia history brought the Flying Circus crashing to earth.

Sin in the City of Brotherly Love

About 9:00 p.m., a small army of plainclothes officers slowly assembled in the vicinity of Vine and Franklin, blending in with the evening crowd. Shortly before ten o'clock, the signal was given, and the plainclothesmen blockaded every door of the Palace. Suddenly, a phalanx of uniformed officers stormed the building, using their riot sticks to corral customers and employees. They were assisted by members of Applegate's in-house police squad, who deserted their patron once they realized the jig was up.

The Palace of Flying Animals quickly became a house of horrors as panicked men and women tried to hide under booths or crawl out through smashed windows. "The shrieks of frightened women sounded above the loud tones of the big steam organ," reported the *Inquirer*, "which continued in operation long after the 'flying horses' had been deserted by their riders." Screams echoed throughout the Tenderloin that night, as the police raided other brothels on Cherry and Franklin Streets.

According to the *Inquirer*, 106 females and 109 males were arrested at Applegate's Palace alone. Among them were numerous minors, including a class of nautical students from the school ship *Saratoga*, a group of girls aged ten to sixteen and Chippy Patterson, son of prominent corporate lawyer C. Stuart Patterson, who had dropped in to celebrate his seventeenth birthday just before the police crashed the party. Three patrol wagons shuttled back and forth between the Palace and City Hall for hours. It was midnight when the last prisoner was brought before the judge and after 5:00 a.m. when the magistrate finished hearing the witnesses.

Stripped of his official protection, James R. Applegate was charged with "keeping a disorderly house and with harboring minors in an establishment where they met those of the opposite sex for the purpose of adjourning to houses of a questionable character." After being told by the judge that he was "a curse to the city," Applegate was ordered to post $1,000 bail, plus an additional $1,500 on a separate assault charge pressed by Mary Mills, one of his employees. Applegate's thirty-two-year-old son Frank was released on $600 bail.

Despite this show of moral force, the circus animals were flying again the next day. After a bondsman posted $2,500 as security, Applegate was allowed to reopen his establishment. The indignant proprietor told the newspapers that the police action was "an outrage" and that he was considering suing the city. He complained that his poor son Frank had lost his reason after spending ten hours in a jail cell. The *Inquirer* sympathized, editorializing that the police had overstepped their authority and that it was unnecessary "to raid and arrest all the spectators [who] had a perfect right to be there."

Applegate pleaded not guilty to keeping a disorderly house and to assaulting Mary Mills and "soliciting her to commit a nameless offense." His trial date was fixed for mid-February. In preparation, both the prosecution and the defense hired numerous detectives to dig up as much dirt on the other side as possible. Two weeks after the raid, a dozen girls arrested at Applegate's, aged sixteen to nineteen, still languished in City Hall jail cells (girls younger than sixteen had been sent to either the almshouse or the Magdalen Society). Detectives grilled these teenagers relentlessly, trying to make them confess that they were prostitutes and that Applegate was their pimp. Meanwhile, Applegate continued to operate his Palace of Flying Animals, although under police watch to ensure that the public peace was not disturbed.

The police were not watching very closely because trouble continued to stalk the Palace. On February 12, two men seeking to ride the carousel got into a brawl with Applegate and one of the "special" officers assigned to keep order. Both customers were so badly wounded that they had to be rushed to Hahnemann Hospital. The next week, eighteen-year-old Maggie McLain, a Palace habitué, was reported missing. Her parents insinuated that Maggie had committed suicide after being seduced by another Palace regular, a man twice her age. Meanwhile, newspaper ads continued to tout Applegate's Grand Palace of Flying Animals as "a $150,000 playhouse for the Children—Free, with free candy."

Applegate's trial was postponed throughout the spring as his lawyers filed motion after motion. When these failed, Applegate took to his bed with "acute nervous prostration." His physicians testified that the sixty-eight-year-old man—who had beaten two customers into bloody pulps with his cane a short time before—was now at death's door, unable to walk, sleep or eat. After numerous delays, Applegate's trial was firmly fixed for Monday, May 9, 1892.

Shortly after midnight on Saturday, May 7, 1892, a fire of unknown origin broke out at Applegate's Palace. The vast wooden structure burned to the ground in less than half an hour. Unable to save the Palace, firemen focused on preserving the First Moravian Church next door, which suffered slight damage to its roof. Applegate, who rushed to the scene with his attorney, estimated that his losses would be about $40,000, of which insurance would cover less than half. He also announced that he would build another amusement hall on the site. When First Moravian Church congregants arrived for service Sunday morning, they were stunned (and probably thrilled) to find a scorched field where their troublesome neighbor had stood the week before.

Two days after the fire, the judge in the Applegate case told a stunned courtroom that the accused had offered a conditional plea of guilty, promising not to rebuild his Palace if he were discharged with a suspended sentence. The district attorney said that he was "obliged" to accept this offer. His rationale was that since many of the young girls arrested at the Palace had been restored to their families, their chances for respectable lives would be destroyed if they were called as witnesses and forced to confess their sins publicly. The district attorney also announced that he was loath, in the interest of public morals, to spread the scandalous details of the conduct of Palace customers. The judge threatened to sentence Applegate to jail if he did not behave in the future and then set him free. Philadelphia's reputation as the city that provided the finest justice money could buy was upheld once again.

On July 17, 1892, the First Moravian Church held its final service at Franklin and Wood Streets. It would occupy temporary quarters until its new Fairmount Avenue church was ready in March 1893. The week before, Applegate had sold his mortgage on the church property to a manufacturer of ladies' dress trimmings. When the factory foundations were dug in September 1892, seven forgotten coffins from the First Moravian Churchyard were uncovered. As five hundred spectators watched, the workmen chopped the bones and wood into small pieces with their shovels and then carted them away. Today, the Vine Street Expressway has obliterated any traces of Applegate's Palace and the First Moravian Church.

Although Applegate seemed to have gotten off scot-free, the destruction of his Palace of Flying Animals marked the beginning of his downfall. Haunted by his reputation as a ravisher of young girls, Applegate opened a New York studio in 1893, leaving his business at Eighth and Vine in his son's hands. He was back in Philadelphia within eighteen months. But Frank Applegate refused to associate with his father and moved to New Jersey with his mother. During this period, James Applegate's two adult daughters died, one of smallpox and the other of scarlet fever.

In 1903, James Applegate also moved to New Jersey, setting up a photographic studio on East State Street in Trenton. According to the *Trenton Times*, "He was a man of retiring disposition and made but few friends while in Trenton." The following year, there appears to have been a second, unspecified scandal; the *Times* discreetly stated that "Applegate is said to have again attracted attention by his habits." Shortly afterward, the photographer vanished.

In April 1911, a frail, elderly man, dressed in rags, was brought into the Central Police Court in Philadelphia after being arrested for vagrancy. The court officials were stunned to learn that the tramp was one-time millionaire James R. Applegate. A few months earlier, Applegate had also been jailed in Los Angeles on vagrancy charges. The city's mayor had contacted several Pennsylvania congressmen in Washington, who had raised money for Applegate to return home. The old man had boarded a train for the East in February, only to vanish for two months once he reached Chicago. Somehow, the eighty-seven-year-old derelict had managed to find his way back to Philadelphia.

The court officials and detectives took up another collection to send Applegate to Hammonton, New Jersey, where his son Frank lived. As the pile of pocket change grew, Applegate reportedly stopped them. "Don't overdo it, boys," he said. "You probably know others who are more deserving, and I am thankful for what you've already done."

A police sergeant escorted Applegate to Broad Street Station, where he boarded a Pennsylvania Railroad train to New Jersey. Whether he ever reconnected with his son or simply disappeared somewhere along the thirty miles between Philadelphia and Hammonton is unknown. When the train left the station, James R. Applegate—photographic innovator, amusement impresario, political operator, publican, pimp and procurer—disappeared from the pages of Philadelphia history forever.

MY MOTHER, THE "COUNTESS"

The Anita de Bettencourt Fraud, 1892

*The Countess is not prepossessing in appearance, being short, stout and dark,
but she has a very attractive and gracious manner. Her new-made friends were
unanimous in voting her a most charming hostess.*
—*"A Countess and Her Millions,"* Philadelphia Inquirer, *October 31, 1892*

Shortly after midnight on January 16, 1906, a woman's screams pierced
the silence of North Marshall Street, ricocheting off the brownstones that
lined the quiet block in the Northern Liberties. Stunned into consciousness,
a few neighbors leaned out of their windows, shivering in the winter night.
But when they located the source of the ruckus, they returned to their beds,
wrapping pillows around their heads to muffle the panicked cries.

As usual, the screams were emanating from 623 North Marshall. Residents
of the street were inured to the frequent late-night rows between seventy-five-
year-old Anita McMurrow, a boarder there, and her son John, a mean drunk
in his mid-thirties. Only two nights earlier, Mrs. McMurrow had banged
on a neighbor's door at midnight, dressed in her nightgown and begging
for protection from her abusive child. This time, however, Mrs. McMurrow
did not flee. Once her screams had died away, her son John—a large, flabby
man with a sad face and walrus moustache—left the house and staggered
into the night.

Two hours later, the block was reawakened by more screams from 623
North Marshall. Now it was Jane Herron, Mrs. McMurrow's housekeeper.
"She's dead! She's dead!" the hysterical woman shrieked from the second-
floor window. "For God's sake, some of you come and break in the door!"

This time the neighbors responded, racing upstairs to the McMurrows' apartment. In the bedroom they found Anita McMurrow—a short, stocky woman with a square, masculine face—fully dressed and seated beside her bed with her legs splayed out. Her white hair was disheveled, her neck was bruised and her features were contorted with pain and fear. And she was very dead.

A short time later, John McMurrow returned home with a box of candy. Filled with guilt over assaulting his mother, he had gone out—leaving her battered but alive—to buy a make-up present. He appeared as stunned as his neighbors to find his mother dead. Later that morning, John was arrested and taken to the police station at Tenth and Buttonwood Streets to await trial for homicide.

Surprisingly, the sordid death of this otherwise obscure woman made headlines across the United States. Newspapers screamed the details of her demise not only in Philadelphia but also in New York, Baltimore, Chicago and San Jose. For the world had once known Anita McMurrow as the "Countess de Bettencourt," self-proclaimed heiress to $32 million in Spanish bonds and vast estates in Cuba. In the Centennial year of 1876, she had entertained the American president and the emperor of Brazil at her mansion.

Years later, the countess was revealed as a massive fraud, funding her lavish lifestyle with money taken from hundreds of "investors" who hoped to be compensated richly once her claims were recognized by Spain. The Spanish minister to America had committed suicide in 1883, supposedly because he improperly loaned government funds to the "noblewoman." Countless other bankruptcies, breakdowns and suicides were attributed to her two decades of swindling.

The origins of the "countess" are shrouded in mystery, since she told a slightly different story to everyone she conned. The woman known as "Anita de Bettencourt" was born in Cuba, or Barcelona or Madrid sometime around 1830. She first appeared in Philadelphia in the 1860s, working as a dishwasher in a boardinghouse at Second and Race Streets. She had two small children and was known as Mrs. Folsom, although there was no sign of a Mr. Folsom. Anita explained that her husband was a ship captain lost when his vessel sank off the coast of India, although she never disclosed the name of his ship or the date of its wreck.

Soon after Anita's arrival in Philadelphia, her daughter died. A boarder at Second and Race, a sailmaker named John McMurrow, paid for the little girl's funeral and comforted the distraught widow. In 1870, the couple married and moved to a house on West Montgomery Avenue with Anita's

The Countess de Bettencourt (aka Mrs. Anita McMurrow), con woman extraordinaire, wearing the Order of the Golden Rose she supposedly received from Pope Leo XIII.

surviving child, William. Within a few years, the McMurrows had their own child, a boy named John after his father. Now respectably married with a home and a steady (if limited) income from John's job at the Navy Yard, Anita McMurrow was a proud member of Philadelphia's petite bourgeoisie. But this was only the first step for the ambitious and amoral woman.

Around 1874, the former kitchen drudge announced to her startled neighbors that she was really the Countess de Bettencourt, a Cuban native whose late parents were Spanish grandees of the purest Castilian blood. She explained that her older brother had disposed of his vast estates in Cuba before his death, investing his money in Spanish bonds. As his sole surviving relative, Countess Anita was heir to a fortune worth $32 million in U.S. dollars (the equivalent of $525 million today).

But because of problems with the notoriously corrupt Spanish government, she was unable to gain access to her estate. If some of her friends could lend her the paltry sum of a few thousand dollars so her lawyers could advance her claim, then she would compensate them handsomely once her suit was won. As proof of her story, the countess displayed a huge safe filled with deeds and documents plastered with wax seals and written in Spanish. Luckily for Anita, few Philadelphians could read Spanish.

Many of her neighbors, as well as the merchants she patronized, responded with loans of $2,500, $5,000 or more. The equivalent of $50,000 or $100,000 today, these sums often constituted the lenders' life savings. But the countess's supporters were confident that the grateful noblewoman would repay them many times over once her legal wrangles were resolved.

How could so many people be taken in by such a far-fetched story? Like most successful swindlers, the countess was a charismatic, compelling personality. Despite her ignoble appearance—she was short, stout and

North Broad Street in 1876, lined with the mansions of Philadelphia's newly rich. For nearly twenty years, this was the Countess de Bettencourt's hunting grounds.

swarthy, with a hawk-like nose and a square jaw—the countess could seduce any man with her vivacity and charm. She never hustled or begged but simply let it be known that she was mildly inconvenienced and that any assistance would be handsomely rewarded.

Most importantly, the Countess de Bettencourt was just one of many rags-to-riches figures who appeared in America during this period, like gilt-edged butterflies emerging from middle-class cocoons. Philadelphia, the "workshop of the world," spawned dozens of millionaires in the industrial boom during and after the Civil War. Its poster child was P.A.B. Widener. A butcher before the Civil War, Widener was one of the wealthiest men in America by 1880, with interests in trolleys, tobacco, steel, oil and steamships. He and his partner, a former grocer named William Elkins, lived in gigantic gingerbread mansions that faced each other across North Broad Street, the Champs-Élysées of Philadelphia's nouveaux riches.

In the midst of so many Cinderella stories, why couldn't a dishwasher be reborn as a Spanish countess? Those who lent her money—the striving shopkeepers, butchers and clerks of North Philadelphia—saw the charming, accessible Countess de Bettencourt as their ticket to both Philadelphia high society and the loftier realms of European royalty. Who wouldn't sacrifice their life savings if it meant that one day they would waltz with Spanish nobles in P.A.B. Widener's glittering ballroom?

Thanks to these loans, the countess and her family lived like true grandees. In 1875, they rented two adjoining houses on Twenty-second Street between Diamond and Norris, then an affluent neighborhood. The countess joined the houses to create a thirty-room mansion decorated in the latest Moorish fashion, with an inner courtyard in the Castilian style. The walls were lined with age-darkened portraits of Spanish nobles, whom the countess identified as her ancestors. Her household staff consisted of ten female servants, five male servants and two Catholic priests. A fine carriage was always waiting outside her door, since the stout countess refused to go anywhere on foot.

The countess entertained frequently and lavishly, adorned with diamonds that she claimed were a gift from King Alfonso XII of Spain. Her guests included Francisco Barca, Spanish minister plenipotentiary to the United States, and his secretary, Jose Philippi Segrario. In 1876, during the opening of the Centennial Exposition, the countess threw a reception for President Ulysses S. Grant and Emperor Dom Pedro of Brazil, attended by the cream of Philadelphia society.

The countess traveled frequently to Europe, ostensibly to negotiate the recovery of her fortune with King Alfonso. After one voyage, she returned wearing a large golden brooch shaped like a flower, studded with precious stones. This, she explained, was the Order of the Golden Rose, bestowed upon her by Pope Leo XIII during a visit to the Vatican. Such an order has existed since the eighth century to honor female supporters of the Catholic faith. Whether the countess acquired her rose from the pope or from a jewelry store is one of the many mysteries surrounding her.

The countess operated her scam successfully throughout the 1880s. Her friendship with the Spanish ministers Barca and Segrario gave her credibility, as well as access to wealthier "contributors." Gradually, her investor base spread to New York and Washington, and the size of her requests for assistance grew to $50,000.

The countess took a few tumbles along her triumphant progress. The McMurrows moved often during the 1880s, leaving their Moroccan palace on Twenty-second Street for Sixteenth Street, then Fifteenth and Jefferson, then Diamond Street and finally 2220 North Broad Street. These frequent relocations suggest that they were trying to stay one step ahead of their creditors. In 1883, Francisco Barca, the Spanish minister and close associate of the countess, put a bullet through his brain in a New York hotel room. Although the reasons for his death were suppressed, there were whispers about financial improprieties involving government funds "lent" to the countess.

When Grover Cleveland was elected president in 1885, the countess commissioned a local jeweler to craft a silver inkstand in the shape of a ship and send it to the White House with her card. The president replied with a cordial note of thanks, which the countess used to persuade new pigeons to bankroll her. Unfortunately, she did not share any of her fresh funds with the jeweler, who, after a year of having his bills ignored, threatened to send the invoice directly to President Cleveland. His was one of the few debts the countess actually paid.

By 1890, many of the countess's lenders were demanding repayment, fed up by fifteen years of no return on their investments. Rumors abounded of desperate creditors driven to the brink: Louis Egbert lost his mind, as well as his savings, and was committed to the Norristown Insane Asylum. Benjamin Crabtree lent the countess over $50,000, went bankrupt and moved west to start over. Rafael Avenido of New Orleans died of a broken heart after losing his whole fortune of $40,000. Many creditors were represented by John G. Johnson, the city's foremost lawyer and art collector, but he was unable to persuade them to press criminal charges.

Finally, one of the countess's victims took action. On October 29, 1892, Anita McMurrow was charged with obtaining $2,500 from William Toplis, a Germantown pharmacist, upon false representation. When the case came to trial in early November, the courtroom was packed with the countess's other victims. Newspaper reporters delighted in pointing out that most of these people had come on foot, while the countess and her husband arrived in their usual carriage. These trusting souls gasped audibly when Spanish officials testified that Anita McMurrow's claims to a Cuban fortune were completely false, as was her title. Many of them had just realized that their life savings were gone forever.

When William Toplis took the stand, he testified that he had traveled to New York City with the countess, a family friend, in 1891. She had escorted him to the Mercantile Trust & Safe Deposit Company at 120 Broadway. There, she introduced him to bank secretary Elmer Billings, who called the countess "the wealthiest woman in the world," with an income of $5,500 a day. Billings showed Toplis two large vaults, where the countess supposedly stored her $32 million in Spanish bonds. Billings then told Toplis that in exchange for a $2,500 loan to the countess, the bank would hire him as a bookkeeper, even though the pharmacist had no financial experience. Once the loan was made, however, Toplis heard nothing further from Billings.

The next day, Toplis's lawyer caused a sensation when he had Billings's letters to the countess read aloud in court, disclosing the romantic relationship between the widowed bank secretary and the sixty-one-year-old married noblewoman. "My own darling Anita," one letter gushed, "How I would like to hug you and feel your warm love!" In another missive, Billings panted, "I leave a kiss here for you, and will think of you lovingly till I see you. Elmer, true to death." Testifying in his own defense, Billings explained that he was just expressing gratitude to the countess for taking care of his late mother: "She was a little old, that is true, but I loved her because she loved Mother. I returned her affection, but there was nothing familiar."

Shortly afterward, the case concluded. The charge of obtaining money under false pretenses was dismissed, but the countess and Billings were each charged with conspiracy and forced to pay fines of several thousand dollars. While Anita McMurrow had escaped imprisonment and serious damages, her long-running grift was over. She had been exposed to the world as a complete fraud, and the newspaper headlines about her now put quotation marks around "countess." Her husband had been fired from his job, and other creditors were lining up to file charges. The McMurrows closed up 2220 North Broad Street, sold what they could, put the rest in storage and disappeared.

Six years later, in 1898, a small advertisement ran in Philadelphia newspapers:

> *ANITA DE BETTENCOURT MCMURROW is hereby notified that her goods will be sold at auction November 30, unless settlement is first made.*
> *ATLAS STORAGE CO.*

The liquidation notice reawakened interest in the bogus countess. The *Inquirer* published an article that described how Anita McMurrow was living quietly in Philadelphia with her husband and her "only living child, William" (ignoring her younger son, John, who was very much alive). In a putative interview with William McMurrow, the loyal son declared "that there has been nothing dishonest about my mother's claim against Spain and that she has done nothing of which to be ashamed." The family was not in financial distress, and the storage company had been paid. William insisted that his mother "never represented herself as a countess," despite years of newspaper coverage to the contrary.

After 1898, the McMurrows vanished again until 1904, when an *Inquirer* article crowed "Bogus Countess Reappears!" The recently widowed Anita McMurrow had returned to Philadelphia after living in Maryland for several years. Thanks to a small pension she had received upon her husband's death, she was finally able to redeem her household goods, mostly family portraits and personal papers, from storage. Soon afterward, the *Inquirer* reported that the "countess" was being sued by a doctor for an unpaid bill of $630.

After two years of quiet desperation, the "countess" made her farewell appearance in the media in January 1906. At the coroner's inquest into her death, a portrait emerged of a nearly penniless woman, renting a small apartment on a back street, who still engaged a housekeeper and a secretary to handle her correspondence. The female Svengali who had swindled millions of dollars left an estate valued at eighty-five dollars. Her primary possession was a strongbox that contained her diary, newspaper clippings and pawn tickets for her jewelry, including her papal golden rose. Friends testified that Anita McMurrow had remained cheerful despite frequent assaults by her alcoholic son John. The loving mother had refused to commit John to an asylum or even to report him to the police.

On January 19, the Philadelphia coroner ruled that Anita McMurrow had died from heart disease and not as a result of her son's beating. Released from jail, John McMurrow returned to 623 North Marshall. There, he met his half brother William, who had moved to New York and changed his last name to Folsom. The following day, hundreds of curiosity seekers swarmed around the house to witness the funeral, almost trampling the maid to view Mrs. McMurrow's body in the front parlor. Despite the mob, only twelve mourners accompanied the coffin to New Cathedral Cemetery at Second and Butler Streets, where the countess rests today in an unmarked grave.

A few months after Anita McMurrow's death, an eerie postscript to her story emerged. In June 1906, the body of Mrs. Joanna E. Forster was recovered from the Delaware River near the Chestnut Street wharf. Mrs. Forster had once owned 623 North Marshall Street, and Mrs. McMurrow had been her boarder. The two women were devoted friends, and Mrs. Forster had been only too willing to lend money to the impoverished countess. Perhaps because of her generosity, she had been forced to sell the Marshall Street house and move in with her son in Darby.

Her son insisted that Mrs. Forster had been taking the ferry to visit a daughter in Trenton and had fallen overboard. But the coroner believed that Mrs. Forster had been trying to starve herself to death for some time; failing to do so, she had gone to the river and drowned herself. Unable to agree, the jury rendered an open verdict of "death from drowning." So the world will never know if Joanna Forster was the final victim of the smiling, seductive sociopath known as the Spanish countess.

THE FRAYED FABRIC OF OUR LIVES

The Storey Cotton Con, 1905

Would YOU be satisfied with an income of 6 per cent and upward each month from the use of your spare cash if it could be safely invested where you were SURE of at least that result and KNEW POSITIVELY that your money was always available and being handled by a reputable and reliable house? If so, write for proof.
—*Storey Cotton Company brochure*

Beginning in 1900, thousands of Americans received handsome brochures from a Philadelphia investment firm that promised them the unbeatable combination of high returns and absolute safety. The Storey Cotton Company, headquartered in the elegant new Bourse Building on South Fifth Street, specialized in cotton futures and contracts—innovative and esoteric financial instruments that few people then understood, even on Wall Street.

But everyone wore cotton, as the brochure explained, and the United States was the world's largest producer of the commodity. Tables of complex statistics were balanced by photographs of cotton fields and knitting mills, illustrating the real wealth backing the investments. Readers were assured that the Storey Cotton Company's well-placed financial experts were privy to confidential, inside information that ensured the firm's consistent returns, year after year.

Around the country, thousands of ordinary Americans read the honeyed words and succumbed to temptation. They withdrew their hard-earned savings from their banks or from under their beds, mailed it to the Storey Cotton Company and waited anxiously. And a month later, they received a check for

One of the many handsome brochures sent by the Storey Cotton Company to thousands of ordinary Americans from 1900 until its collapse in 1905.

6 percent of their initial investment. From then on, monthly dividends arrived without fail: $6, $8, even $10, for every $100 invested.

The ecstatic shareholders poured every cent they owned into Storey Cotton, even mortgaging their houses. They wrote glowing endorsements, which were quoted in Storey brochures and newspaper ads. They formed investment clubs to pool their resources and purchase more shares. They recommended Storey Cotton to their friends, receiving a 10 percent commission on each account they referred.

These small-town strivers—whose yearly incomes were numbered in hundreds rather than thousands of dollars—felt that they had finally boarded the financial gravy train that was transporting turn-of-the-century America to prosperity. Soon, they would be wealthy enough to afford a house with electricity and indoor plumbing, to let their children finish high school rather than work or even to purchase the ultimate plaything of the rich: an automobile. But they would have felt much less optimistic if they had known what was really happening to their life savings in the Bourse Building.

Years before the infamous swindler Charles Ponzi lent his name to this particular kind of confidence game, the Storey Cotton Company was a classic Ponzi scheme, where the organizers counted on their victims' covetousness overwhelming their common sense. These "get-rich-quick men" promised unrealistically large and consistent returns, which they paid from their investors' own money rather than from genuine profits. Needless to say, a healthy sum always remained in the swindlers' pockets.

Get-rich-quick men explained their sky-high returns by spouting technical jargon about new financial instruments or citing their managers' unparalleled acumen. At first, the swindlers paid dividends religiously to keep the original investors hooked and to attract new ones, since a constantly increasing cash flow was vital to keep the fraud afloat. These schemes usually fell apart when the promoters a) ran out of money; b) took the money and ran; or c) ended up in jail when someone blew the whistle. If all of this sounds familiar, it's what Mr. Bernard Madoff is alleged to have done from roughly 1990 until December 2008.

The five principals of the Storey Cotton Company—as well as the Provident Investment Bureau, an affiliated firm that supposedly paid 50 percent interest a year on its deposit certificates—were, on the surface, upstanding civic leaders. Beneath their respectable veneers, they were as crooked a band of grifters as has ever joined forces in America, with nearly twenty criminal aliases among them.

Their ringleader was Judge Franklin T. Stone, a churchgoer and philanthropist who lived with his family at 437 South Forty-fourth

The mansion of Judge Franklin Stone (aka Frank Marrin) at 437 South Forty-fourth Street in West Philadelphia, as it appeared in 1951. *Philadelphia City Archive.*

Street in West Philadelphia. In reality, Stone was Frank C. Marrin, a Brooklyn lawyer who had disappeared in 1894 after bilking an elderly widow out of $70,000. After that, he ran scams in Chicago, San Francisco and New Orleans before settling in Philadelphia as "Judge Stone" around 1900. Stone had no official connection with Storey Cotton, although he served as its general manager under another alias, Thomas Harper.

In Chicago, Stone had hooked up with Sophie Beck, a small-town girl with a trim figure, a steel-trap mind and a taste for luxury. The two had lived as husband and wife for several years, but by the time they reached Philadelphia their relationship was purely professional. As "Estelle Collins," Sophie served as head stenographer for Storey Cotton, drawing the princely salary of $500 a month in addition to her share of the profits. She lived in a Chestnut Hill mansion with her real husband, Richard Graham, a handsome young wagon driver she had acquired when he delivered hay to her summer estate in Jenkintown.

Stanley Francis, alias Arthur S. Foster-Francis, was British-born. Besides his connections to the Storey Cotton Company and Provident Investment Bureau, Francis ran the United States Trust Company at 20 South Third Street. He lived in style at 4601 Cedar Avenue in West Philadelphia, a few blocks from Marrin. He liked to boast that he came from a noble English family and that his brother was the military governor of the Fiji Islands. In the 1890s, this "nobleman" had served jail time in New Orleans for organizing investment scams.

William Henry Lattimer, manager of the Provident Investment Bureau, was a card shark, gambler and bigamist. Born in Wilkes-Barre, "Handsome Harry" Lattimer was the town's most dashing sport, with the face and figure of an Adonis. He also possessed a lengthy rap sheet for running floating crap and poker games throughout Northeastern Pennsylvania. Despite the existence of one long-suffering wife and two children, Lattimer had seduced and "married" at least two other women.

F. Ewart Storey (alias Oliver Quinlan) was another "British nobleman" and putative president of the Storey Cotton Company. Although he lent his name to the enterprise, Storey kept the lowest profile of the five swindlers, with little known about his personal life.

The Storey Cotton Company and Provident Investment Bureau were only two of the many fraudulent brokerage firms, or "bucket shops," that populated the Bizarro World known as Philadelphia finance at the time. A bucket shop, the nineteenth-century equivalent of a boiler room operation, drew its name from the low-class pubs of Dickensian England that drained other saloons' discarded kegs and sold the dregs in buckets for a penny.

The Bourse Building on South Fifth Street as it appeared in 1905, when it was Philadelphia's financial nerve center and home to Storey Cotton Company.

In his 1904 exposé of urban politics, *The Shame of the Cities*, journalist Lincoln Steffens described Philadelphia as "corrupt and contented." The city's amoral political and business atmosphere—where everything went so long as the right palms were greased—made it a mecca for bucket shops, which devoured $100 million of Americans' hard-earned money each year while rarely trading a stock.

Philadelphia's bucket shops operated like the basement betting parlor in the Newman-Redford film *The Sting*. In the paneled offices out front, clients sat in comfortable armchairs and watched clerks update prices on a huge blackboard, the changes relayed to them by managers monitoring clattering stock tickers. Other clerks manned telephones and telegraphs, receiving orders from off-site clients. Attractive young secretaries—"glib of tongue and profuse of promises," according to the *Inquirer*—offered clients cigars and drinks.

In the back rooms, an army of unseen clerks created the illusion that the bucket shop was a legitimate brokerage. They jotted down stock prices lifted from a valid exchange via an illegal telegraph line (Frank Marrin's brother Thomas ran the "Marrin Pirate Wire," the largest source of stolen stock data). They then "adjusted" the quotes before feeding them into the front office ticker, depending on whether the company was bullish or bearish on the stock. Sometimes they simply made up prices. Their goal was to entice clients (most of whom bought on margin) to load up on "hot" issues that would then plummet mysteriously, enabling the bucket shop to close their accounts and keep their money.

Other clerks manufactured the paper trail of buy and sell orders, cancelled checks and margin calls to prove that a trade had been executed, in case an indignant customer demanded evidence. To complete the illusion of legitimacy, Philadelphia's bucket shops created their own sham stock exchange, the Consolidated (conveniently located in the Bourse), to bypass the legitimate Philadelphia Stock Exchange. At the Consolidated, more clerks painstakingly fabricated the documents, which showed that for every five hundred shares bought of Baldwin Locomotive, another five hundred shares had been sold. In rare cases, the Consolidated Stock Exchange actually traded shares to validate a deal, but this was always its last resort.

This carefully crafted system flourished under an official aegis of neglect and bribery. There was no government oversight of the stock or commodity markets. The Federal Reserve System would not exist until 1913, and the Securities and Exchange Commission would not be created until 1934. In 1900, the only guardian of the financial markets was the U.S. Postal Service, charged with protecting the public from fraudulent materials dispatched via the mails and newspapers. But since many postal inspectors were on the bucket shops' payrolls, most complaints from defrauded consumers ended up in the Dead Letter Office.

For five years, the game operated like clockwork, and the triumvirate of the Storey Cotton Company, Provident Investment Bureau and United States Trust Company flourished. The three interconnected shells raked in over a million dollars a year in investments and deposits, more than enough to pay dividends and interest while making their managers extremely wealthy. Judge Franklin Stone kept a stable of thoroughbred racing horses in Lexington, Kentucky. Stanley Francis bought his pretty young wife a shiny red motorcar. "Handsome Harry" Lattimer played the country squire at his Wilkes-Barre estate. Sophie Beck set her boy-toy husband up as president of his own gas company, with an annual salary of $50,000. They were happy, their investors were happy and the legion of government officials on the take was very, very happy.

And then a muckraking journalist named Merrill A. Teague had to come along and spoil everything. In early 1905, Teague launched a series of articles in the *North American* newspaper, exposing Philadelphia's spider's web of bucket shops, sham exchanges and crooked officials. The unholy trinity of Storey Cotton, Provident Investment and United States Trust received star billing. "Judge Franklin Stone" was exposed as the swindler Frank Marrin, whose brother operated the biggest illegal wire racket in the country. Unsavory details emerged about the other managers, including jail terms, abandoned spouses and other frauds.

At first, the managers took the high road, ignoring the articles and continuing to pay dividends. If customers questioned them, they implied that Teague's smears were payback for not advertising in the *North American*. The few customers who insisted on closing out were paid in full, prompting many of them to reopen their accounts. When Teague's exposés continued to appear, the managers' expensive attorneys threatened the *North American* with libel suits.

Meanwhile, advertisements appeared in hundreds of newspapers around the country, encouraging potential customers to "listen to this statement of facts: for many years investors in cotton have been paid every month large and sure profits earned safely by the 'Storey Method'; never a dollar lost, capital always subject to withdrawal subject to terms of contract." Existing customers were inundated with circulars, offering them special access for a limited time to a fresh issue of Storey Cotton stock that paid even higher rates of interest. Desperate for cash, the Storey gang was selling harder than ever before.

But the hemorrhaging had begun. Teague's articles ran throughout the winter of 1905, revealing the full extent of the Storey/Provident scam. As his disclosures were picked up by newspapers around the country, new investments slowed to a trickle while requests for redemption soared. The elegant offices of the Storey Cotton Company and Provident Investment Bureau were filled with angry customers, demanding their money in person after having their letters and telegrams ignored. Even the "respectable" United States Trust Company showed signs of a run by panicked customers.

In mid-March, the Storey Cotton Company suddenly closed its Bourse Building office. A few days later, the Provident Investment Bureau also shut its doors. Receivers were appointed by the United States District Court to review the companies' finances and repay their clients. When the receivers searched the abandoned offices of both firms, they found hundreds of unopened letters from customers begging for their money. An initial audit concluded that Storey Cotton, with over ten thousand customers, had assets of $20,000 and liabilities of over $250,000. Provident Investment, with more than one thousand customers, had over $1 million in outstanding claims but only $3,300 in assets. Further investigation revealed that neither company had ever made any transactions in either cotton or corporate stocks.

The government focused on tracking down the principals of the failed companies. On March 24, Stanley Francis was arrested at his offices in the eponymous Francis Building at 420 Sansom Street, triggering the collapse of his United States Trust Company. But thanks to a tip from a friendly postal inspector, the other principals had all vanished. Government agents scoured the Northeast, keeping a close watch on train stations and piers.

But the rest of the "Storey gang" was already en route to Europe. Investigators realized that Sophie Beck —who, as Estelle Collins, had been

GET-RICH-QUICK WOMAN IN HIDING

The beautiful and brilliant Sophie Beck, the "million-dollar stenographer" who masterminded much of the Storey Cotton Company scam and engineered the principals' escape.

known heretofore only as the chief stenographer of the Storey Cotton Company—was the real brains behind the combined operations. Once the talented Miss Beck had realized that the crash of both Storey and Provident was inevitable, she had meticulously plotted the escape of the firms' principals (except for Francis, who was left behind to take the fall).

Beck emptied bank accounts, liquidated the firms' remaining assets and mortgaged her colleagues' real estate, raising between $1 and $2 million in cash. Knowing that all ocean liners would be watched, she chartered a private yacht to ferry the principals and their families to Liverpool. Beck understood that the current international laws would not allow extradition for misuse of the mails, the one crime with which the gang could be charged at present.

Thanks to these revelations, Sophie Beck achieved a nationwide notoriety that would not be matched until Bonnie Parker met Clyde Barrow. Newspapers crowned her "the million-dollar stenographer" and "the queen of the confidence women." Sophie, gushed the *Inquirer*, was "a beautiful, fascinating, and wholly attractive woman, with a graceful and willowy figure, with dark, luminous eyes and a wealth of black hair coiled upon her shapely head." The puritanical *Pawtucket Times* branded Sophie with the scarlet letter, sniffing that she had enjoyed "various amours" before marrying her teamster husband.

With most of the guilty parties abroad, authorities tried to seize their personal assets to repay their creditors. Frank Marrin owned dozens of properties in West Philadelphia, Lattimer had a string of farms in Montour County, Stanley Francis owned valuable commercial real estate and Sophie Beck had her Chestnut Hill and Jenkintown residences. But all had either been mortgaged by Beck or encircled with legal barriers by their attorneys. The receivers weren't even able to commandeer Mrs. Stanley Francis's shiny red automobile. Instead, the spirited woman led them on a high-speed chase through lunchtime crowds in Center City, stopping briefly at J.E. Caldwell's to buy jewelry. The next day, the *Inquirer* noted that "Mrs. Stanley Francis must be added to the list of gifted women. She ran away with an automobile without hitting anybody."

As the repercussions from the Storey/Provident crash spread, public amusement faded. Soon, other Philadelphia bucket shops began to close their doors. Federal authorities discovered that Philadelphia's chief postal inspector had received a $1,100 "loan" from Storey. A judge acquitted a drunk and disorderly case upon learning that the prisoner had invested his savings with Storey Cotton, saying that he had suffered enough. In New London, Connecticut, the local agent for Storey Cotton committed suicide with rat poison, having ruined both himself and his friends by promoting the firm. Across the country, thousands of middle-class Americans, many elderly, attempted to deal with their sudden poverty.

Over the following months, reports filtered back to America of how the Storey gang was "living at the most expensive of European hotels" on the life savings of their former clients. Frank Marrin was the toast of Paris, starting a champagne business under yet another alias, Monsieur Stern. "Handsome Harry" Lattimer told his friends that he liked Germany's climate. Sophie Beck and her husband were said to be running an automobile company in Italy. Meanwhile, Stanley Francis languished in a jail cell in Moyamensing Prison under $100,000 bail, as his lawyers filed appeal after appeal. But the federal authorities continued to predict that his fellow miscreants would soon be apprehended, thanks to their expert sleuthing.

As time passed and the furor died down, the rest of the Storey gang drifted back to America. They didn't return because of the "expert sleuthing" of the feds but because they had run out of cash in Europe and decided to take their chances on their home turf.

In January 1906, "Handsome Harry" Lattimer surfaced in Calgary, Canada, with his latest conquest in tow, a former secretary named Mabel Emerson. But after ending up in a dank Canadian prison on yet another scam, he decided to be extradited to America as a witness for the prosecution. This not only allowed him to cut a deal to avoid further charges but also helped him strike back at Frank Marrin. After Lattimer had blown all of his cash in Europe, he had begged his former colleague for a loan to cover passage back to America. Marrin had sneeringly suggested that his former partner "walk back."

In November 1906, Frank Marrin was arrested in a Buffalo hotel and returned to Philadelphia for trial. Ever the bon vivant, Marrin threw a dinner party for a small group of friends (and the U.S. marshal guarding him) upon his arrival at Broad Street Station. When asked why he had registered at the Buffalo hotel as "Johnstone" if he was innocent, Marrin laughed, "Oh, this is a free country and one name is as good as another, isn't it?" But his insouciance vanished when, unable to raise bail, he ended up in Moyamensing Prison with Stanley Francis.

The debonair Marrin was further shaken when he was confronted by prosecution witness "Handsome Harry" Lattimer, who smiled and said, "You see, Frank? I walked back." Lattimer testified that Marrin was the real mastermind behind the Storey and Provident swindles and was granted immunity. He then returned to Calgary, accompanied by the loyal Mabel.

Thanks to his lawyers' appeals, Marrin did not stand trial until October 1907. Despite a pitiful parade of impoverished clients, the cocky Marrin tried to bet on his innocence with the deputy marshal, saying "three to one I'm acquitted." Instead, he was found guilty on three counts of fraud and conspiracy, given a four-year prison sentence and fined $5,000. Released on bail pending an appeal, Marrin vanished yet again, only to be recaptured in a Manhattan saloon in 1908. He was immediately placed on trial in New York for his 1894 embezzlement of funds from the elderly widow who had died of starvation in 1907. In October 1908, Marrin was sentenced to fifteen to twenty years in Sing Sing Prison in upstate New York.

In September 1909, Sophie Beck was arrested with her husband, Richard Graham, and her two-year-old son in Atlantic City. During her trial, Sophie admitted that the millions she and her cohorts had stolen were gone, spent on European hotels, champagne suppers and fine clothes. Sophie swore that she and Richard were broke and wished to lead an honest life. Touched by her motherhood and her apparent sincerity, the judge gave Sophie a slap on the wrist in the form of a $500 fine. The Grahams retired to a modest two-story row house at 5514 Ludlow Street, a far cry from their Chestnut Hill mansion. Richard, the former gas company president, found work as a pipe fitter.

F. Ewart Storey was the one swindler who did not return to America. According to Sophie Beck, he died in an insane asylum in London.

After a flurry of fresh publicity on the tenth anniversary of the Storey/Provident collapse in 1915, the surviving members of the gang faded into obscurity. "Handsome Harry" Lattimer lived as an apparently honest businessman in Calgary for a decade. He returned to Philadelphia in 1919, dying there the following year. The obituary in the *Wilkes-Barre Times* noted discreetly that Harry had enjoyed "a varied career," becoming involved "in speculations that brought his name into public print throughout the entire country and in several foreign countries which he visited."

Sophie Beck, "the queen of the confidence women," died in 1925 at age fifty-one in a Philadelphia hospital following a surgical procedure. Her husband and her older son, James, were by her side; her six-year-old son, Charles, was not. After Sophie's death, Richard moved his family back to Jenkintown.

Frank Marrin was released from Sing Sing in 1915 and was immediately arrested by the Philadelphia authorities to serve a four-year sentence for his role in the Storey and Provident frauds. Before entering Eastern State Penitentiary, the ever-gallant Marrin contributed the last dollar in his possession to a children's charity. It is believed that when Marrin was released from prison, he returned to New York to practice law again.

In October 1926, sixty-four-year-old Stanley Francis was arrested in New York on the old fake directory fraud, a penny-ante grift that involved presenting false bills to businesses for inclusion in nonexistent directories. For presenting a fake thirty-dollar invoice, he was sentenced to sixty days in the workhouse. Given his poverty and the approach of winter, it's possible that Francis set himself up to obtain free room and board in jail. His pretty young wife had driven away in her shiny red motorcar many years before.

In the final accounting, the Storey Cotton Company is believed to have taken in nearly $3.6 million from its 10,800 customers between its incorporation on December 31, 1900, and its collapse in March 1905. More than $3 million went directly into the pockets of the Storey gang. Its investors had to settle for one-eighth of 1 percent of their original investments. So someone who had invested his life savings of $5,000 with Storey Cotton would have ended up with $6.25. Investors in the Provident Investment Bureau did slightly better, receiving roughly one-third of 1 percent of their investments. An investment of $5,000 in Provident would have ended up as $16.50.

Adjusted for inflation, the Storey and Provident swindles add up to between $75 million and $100 million in 2008 dollars. While that amount is impressive, it pales beside the $65 billion allegedly stolen by financier Bernard Madoff during the two decades that his Ponzi scheme was in operation. As of June 30, 2009, Irving Picard, court-appointed trustee for the Madoff case, announced that he had recovered $1.08 billion of assets related to the case. If so, this means that Madoff's investors might receive 1.66 percent of their original investments—or a whopping $83 for every $5,000 invested.

That's more than ten times what Storey Cotton Company investors received in 1905. So who says the U.S. Securities and Exchange Commission, which spends $961 million in taxpayer dollars each year to prevent such frauds, isn't earning its keep?

THE SUGAR DADDY AND THE BROADWAY BUTTERFLY

The Dot King Murder, 1923

The morning papers had come aboard, reassuring citizens…that sugar daddies were still being surprised in love-nests.
—*P.G. Wodehouse,* The Luck of the Bodkins

Although the term "master of the universe" to denote a high-flying financial wizard did not become common parlance until the 1987 publication of Tom Wolfe's *The Bonfire of the Vanities,* John Kearsley Mitchell III was definitely a master of the universe, class of 1923. Like Wolfe's fictional protagonist, bond trader Sherman McCoy, Mitchell found his privileged world shaken by the combination of an inconvenient young woman and an unfortunate accident in the back streets of New York City.

Mitchell, whose home at 227 South Eighteenth Street faced exclusive Rittenhouse Square, was descended from a long line of distinguished Philadelphia physicians. A graduate of St. Paul's School and Princeton University, Mitchell was president of the Philadelphia Rubber Works Company, a well-respected firm that earned record profits as sales of rubber-tired automobiles soared in the early 1920s. His club affiliations were a testament to his social status: he was a member in good standing of the Philadelphia, Rittenhouse, Union League, Racquet, Radnor Hunt and Merion Cricket Clubs, not to mention the State in Schuylkill.

To add the gilt to his gingerbread, the wealthy Mitchell was married to an even wealthier wife: Frances B. Stotesbury, younger daughter of Edward

The John Kearsley Mitchell residence on Rittenhouse Square, seen at far right. The mansion next door belonged to Kearsley's father-in-law, banker Edward T. Stotesbury.

T. Stotesbury. As head of the investment banking firm of Drexel & Company and partner of J.P. Morgan, Stotesbury was one of the richest men in America. When Mitchell married Frances in 1909, Stotesbury's gifts to his daughter included a check for $1 million, jewelry valued at $500,000 and a country estate in Villanova called the Red Rose.

The Mitchell residence at the northeast corner of Eighteenth and Locust Streets was the former rectory for St. Mark's Episcopal Church. Designed by John Notman in 1853, the stately Tudor manse was part of the Stotesbury family enclave on Rittenhouse Square. Across the square was 1925 Walnut Street, the Edward T. Stotesbury town house (although Stotesbury and his second wife, Eva, spent most of their time at Whitemarsh Hall, their suburban estate). Stotesbury also owned the Joseph Harrison mansion next to the Mitchell house, which he lent to nonprofit organizations. Frances's older sister, Edith, lived with her husband, Sydney Emlen Hutchinson, around the corner at 1718 Walnut.

As Mitchell strolled toward the Pennsylvania Railroad train station on a brisk March morning in 1923, he might have been excused for humming a popular song of the day: "I'm Sitting Pretty in a Pretty Little City." He was fifty-one years old, in excellent health, wealthy and well bred, happily married with two children and securely entrenched in Philadelphia's most exclusive social circles.

And, like many men of his age and class, Mitchell had a little friend on the side, hidden away in a New York love nest. That was the real purpose of his "business" trip on March 14, 1923, taken while his wife was wintering at El Mirasol, her father's Palm Beach estate. At the station, Mitchell met his lawyer and confidant, John H. Jackson. As they boarded the express train to New York, they slipped into their aliases:

Mitchell became Mr. John Marshall, a Boston businessman, while Jackson became Mr. Wilson.

Determined to protect his family and himself, Mitchell insisted on these false identities whenever he traveled to New York with Jackson for relaxation. In New York, he always stayed at a former garage at 26 East Thirty-sixth Street, which he had converted to a comfortable bachelor apartment (its official purpose was to house Rubber Works employees traveling on business). With these elaborate pretenses, Mitchell placed physical and psychological barriers between his two worlds: sedate Rittenhouse Square and sordid Times Square.

We may never know how Mitchell first met Dorothy ("Dot") King, one of the many buxom, blue-eyed blondes who made the Roaring Twenties the Golden Age of the Gold Digger. Born Anna Marie Keenan to a poor Irish family in the 1890s, the young girl escaped an unhappy early marriage with a new name and a job as a fashion model. But her real vocation was adorning the Broadway speakeasies of shadowy characters like Arnold Rothstein (the gambler who fixed the 1919 World Series), persuading wealthy patrons to order expensive bootleg champagne.

Dot King (née Anna Marie Keenan), the Broadway Butterfly and ill-fated paramour of Philadelphia millionaire and socialite John Kearsley Mitchell III.

At one of these nightclubs, Dorothy met the distinguished, white-haired "John Marshall." Soon, the infatuated Mr. Marshall installed Dot in an apartment at 114 West Fifty-seventh Street between Sixth and Seventh Avenues, a marginally respectable block off the beaten track. Dot began to appear in expensive clothing and jewels, gifts from her benefactor. This largesse didn't stop her from entertaining other gentlemen callers, including Albert Guimares, a broker involved in shady business ventures, and Draper Daugherty, son of a former U.S. attorney general. But Marshall was the one Dot called her "heavy sugar daddy" in her love letters.

Sin in the City of Brotherly Love

After arriving in New York on March 14, Marshall and Wilson lunched with Dot at her flat. Marshall gave Dot a bouquet of orchids with a diamond and jade bracelet wrapped around their stems. After lunch, Wilson departed, leaving Marshall and Dot alone for the afternoon. That evening, the two men escorted Dot to dinner, returning about midnight. According to the building's elevator operator, Mr. Wilson left shortly thereafter, while Mr. Marshall tarried with Dot until 2:30 a.m.

When Dot King's maid entered the apartment nine hours later, at 11:30 a.m. on Thursday, March 15, she found her mistress still in bed. This was normal, but the fact that Dot was not breathing was a little unusual. The horrified maid called the police, who determined that Dot had been asphyxiated at about 7:00 a.m. by an unknown assailant who had stolen money, jewelry and furs. Their search uncovered a pair of yellow silk men's pajamas stuffed under a sofa cushion, as well as a love letter, postmarked Palm Beach, which began, "Darling Dottie: Only two days before I will be in your arms. I want to see you, O so much! And to kiss your pretty pink toes."

Dorothy's maid and mother told the police about her leading suitors, Guimares and Marshall. While the police interrogated Guimares, a search began for the mysterious Marshall. Meanwhile, New York's tabloids splattered the scandal across their front pages. "Model's Death Showers Fiery Light on Broadway Jackals," screamed the *Daily News*, dubbing Dot King the "Broadway Butterfly," who "lived on the bubbles of life" and "knew not when to say 'no.'" When the lovers' correspondence was released, every newspaper speculated on the identity of Dot King's "heavy sugar daddy."

Once the story broke, Manhattan district attorney Ferdinand Pecora received a call from a Philadelphia lawyer whose client would testify only if his anonymity would be guaranteed. Jackson and Mitchell appeared at Pecora's office and identified themselves as Mr. Wilson and Mr. Marshall. Pecora listened to their testimony and became convinced that Mitchell was not the killer. To protect the Philadelphian's family from "needless humiliation and suffering," Pecora agreed to withhold Mitchell's name from the press.

Unfortunately, Pecora underestimated the cunning determination of New York reporters, who were lying in wait for Mitchell on a follow-up visit to the district attorney's office. On March 25, newspapers across the country trumpeted the true identity of the mysterious Mr. Marshall. Pecora's attempt to protect Mitchell backfired, since many journalists immediately assumed that Stotesbury had bribed the district attorney to hide his son-in-law's guilt. The *Socialist Call* thundered that "this servility and crawling before a millionaire justifies the hot anger of workingmen!"

Like vultures descending on a carcass, scores of reporters soon surrounded Mitchell's residence on Eighteenth Street, his office in the Land Title Building and the Stotesbury estate in Palm Beach. At El Mirasol, Frances Stotesbury Mitchell, ignorant of her husband's affair, awoke to the indescribable experience of learning about Mitchell's mistress and his possible involvement in her murder and then having to field questions on both topics. According to the *New York Times*, she responded with a truly aristocratic sang-froid: "'I know nothing at all about it,' said Mrs. Mitchell with an expressive wave of her hands." When asked if she would go to her husband, she replied, "Why, of course, I will as soon as I learn whether there is any truth in this report. I have entire confidence in Mr. Mitchell."

In Philadelphia, a reporter was finally allowed to enter 227 South Eighteenth Street to interview Mitchell, who seemed mystified by his questions: "The King case? I know nothing about the case other than what I have read in the papers, and must ask you to excuse me from continuing the interview." At 1718 Walnut, Mitchell's sister-in-law, Edith Hutchinson, told another reporter, "Oh, there must be some mistake. I could not believe that he could be that sort of a rounder."

The following evening, Mitchell boarded a train for Washington. There, he met his wife and father-in-law, who had traveled from Palm Beach in their private railroad car. Sadly, no record exists of their post-reunion conversation. Soon after, the Mitchells sailed for an extended vacation in Europe and a long trip down the Nile. Their departure coincided with the introduction of a timely novelty: the Sugar Daddy doll, a little stuffed man in evening clothes. Before long, Dot King's pet name for Mitchell entered the English language as slang for "an elderly man who lavishes gifts on a young woman," to quote the *Oxford English Dictionary*.

With the Mitchells abroad, the New York Police Department continued to search for Dot King's killer. Suspicion centered on Albert Guimares, whom the police believed throttled Dorothy after she refused to give him the jewelry she had received from Mitchell. Guimares was released when two witnesses swore that they were with him the night of Dot's death. In 1929, however, one of these witnesses fell (or was pushed) off a high balcony at a party. With her last breath, she admitted perjuring herself in the King case but died without naming Guimares as the killer. To this day, the Dorothy King case remains officially unsolved.

In May 1924—fourteen months after the Dot King murder—the Mitchell family sailed back to America, hopeful that the scandal had dissipated. Their arrival was greeted with headlines in all of the New York papers, including a front-page photo in the *Daily News*, with the caption, "TRIED TO FORGET—J.K. Mitchell, 'heavy sugar papa' of slain Dot King, returned with wife from Europe yesterday." As *Time* magazine noted, "If a man has anything in his past which he wants to forget, he should never ride on an ocean liner because the ship news reporter will surely rake it up."

Shortly after their return to Philadelphia, the Mitchells left Rittenhouse Square for good, to live year-round in Villanova. In 1925, Edward T. Stotesbury sold both 227 South Eighteenth Street and the adjoining Harrison mansion. Both were demolished the following year for the Penn Athletic Club (today the Parc Rittenhouse).

Unlike Tom Wolfe's imaginary Sherman McCoy, John Kearsley Mitchell did not allow the events of 1923 to unravel his life. He sold the Philadelphia Rubber Works Company to B.F. Goodrich in 1929, making a tidy profit just before the crash. In 1932, a privately published book appeared, written by John C. Hackett, with the comprehensive title *John Kearsley Mitchell III, Millionaire Murderer, "Sweetheart" and Slayer of Anna Marie Keenan, alias "Dot King." A Classic of American Municipal Corruption*. But the book sank without a trace. Perhaps E.T. Stotesbury suppressed it, or perhaps Americans in 1932 had more pressing concerns than a decade-old Jazz Age peccadillo.

The Mitchells had a long and seemingly peaceful life together on the Main Line. John died at the Red Rose in 1949 at the age of seventy-eight; his wife Frances died there the following year. While both of their obituaries in the *New York Times* noted that they once owned a house on Rittenhouse Square, neither article mentioned Dot King.

Despite this lack of acknowledgment, Dorothy King lives on. Her death inspired many books and movies, including S.S. Van Dine's *The Canary Murder Case* (turned into a movie starring Louise Brooks in the Dot King role) and the 1948 film noir classic *Naked City*. In 1995, she even became the subject of a Tom Waits song, "Walk Away," which begins, "Dot King was whittled from the bone of Cain / With a little drop of poison in a red, red blood." As the years have passed, legend has transformed the Broadway Butterfly from a hard-boiled blonde with dubious taste in men into a mysterious, charismatic and desirable creature—a true *femme fatale*.

THE SESQUI SINKS

The World's Fair Fiasco, 1926

There is no doubt of the success of this affair. President Coolidge has officially
accepted the invitation to be present, and both the city and the state stand back of it.
—Time magazine, November 30, 1925

It was meant to be the world's fair to end all world's fairs: a breathtaking fantasy of light and color, a virtuosic display of modernity and innovation, a celebration of liberty to reunite a war-torn globe and a resounding demonstration that Philadelphia represented not only America's past but also its future.

Instead, the 1926 Sesqui-Centennial International Exposition—a graceless name usually shortened to "the Sesqui"—turned out to be a rain-soaked, ill-planned, poorly attended, politically corrupt, financially ruinous mess that most of the world promptly forgot. No other city would suffer such a disgrace as a result of a world's fair until…well, until Philadelphia tried to throw a Bicentennial Exposition fifty years later.

Like many children who grow up bad, the Sesqui was born from the best parentage and nurtured with the highest hopes. In 1916, John Wanamaker—mercantile millionaire, former postmaster general, civic reformer and one of the organizers of the triumphant Centennial of 1876—recommended that Philadelphia host a second international exposition in 1926. That year would mark the 150th anniversary, or sesquicentennial (then spelled sesqui-centennial), of the signing of the Declaration of Independence.

Civic leaders seized on the Sesqui-Centennial as a way to promote the Fairmount (later Benjamin Franklin) Parkway, then under construction. Modeled on the Champs-Élysées in Paris, the massive boulevard sliced through Center City to connect City Hall with Fairmount Park. Upon completion, it would be lined with civic and cultural institutions, leading up to a magnificent art museum atop the former reservoir. What better way to showcase Philadelphia's transformation into the City Beautiful than a Sesqui-Centennial exposition along the parkway?

Philadelphia's plans for a great world's fair were derailed by America's entry into the Great World War in April 1917. They did not resurface until July 1919, when John Wanamaker again proposed an exposition at his eighty-first birthday celebration. Civic leaders rallied behind Wanamaker once more, seeing a fair as a way for Philadelphia to recover from its postwar economic malaise.

In January 1921, Paul Philippe Cret, professor of architecture at the University of Pennsylvania, unveiled his proposed design for a world's fair. Not surprisingly, Cret's plan centered on the parkway, which he had co-designed with fellow French expatriate Jacques Gréber. A triumphal entrance at Logan Square would welcome visitors to the central fairgrounds on the upper parkway. The great neoclassical structures lining the grand boulevard—including a public library, municipal court, civic auditorium and art museum—would be joined by five temporary exposition buildings. Cret's plans called for rebuilding much of the industrial wasteland along both banks of the Schuylkill River as a way to beautify both Center City and West Philadelphia.

Cret's simple yet visionary design won accolades from most civic leaders and newspaper editors. Yet detractors sprang up immediately. Among the loudest was Joseph M. Huston, architect of the state capitol in Harrisburg. Huston insisted that the fair site should be semideveloped League Island Park, in the marshy flatlands at the tip of South Philadelphia, "where there could be reproduced the hanging gardens of Babylon and where the navies of the world could ride at ease at the gates." Other community leaders jumped into the fray, anxious to win the jobs and development a world's fair would bring to their neighborhoods.

While local boosters squabbled and civic leaders urged action, Mayor J. Hampton Moore equivocated. After much prodding, the mayor authorized $50,000 in seed money for fair planning. The City Council pledged an additional appropriation of $5 million. The mayor and City Council spent the next two years fighting over who should control the fair's money and management. Meanwhile, John Wanamaker, the guiding force behind the fair, died in 1922. Disgusted civic leaders resigned in droves from the Sesqui-Centennial Exhibition Association, the fair planning board. Congress, irritated by the city's inaction, began to debate rescinding its official approval.

This inertia changed to hyperactivity when W. Freeland Kendrick, a major world's fair booster, was elected mayor of Philadelphia in 1923. The new mayor assumed leadership of the Sesqui-Centennial Exhibition Association. Kendrick, a suave and charismatic politician who was considered the best-dressed man in Philadelphia, insisted that the Sesqui would run from June 1 to December 1, 1926. Kendrick also fixed the Sesqui's location at League Island Park, one thousand acres of sparsely populated wetlands that sprawled on both sides of Broad Street between Oregon Avenue and the Navy Yard.

Like everything else in Philadelphia, Kendrick's choice was politically motivated. The fair site was deep in the heart of the First Congressional District, fiefdom of U.S. congressman William S. Vare, "Duke of South Philadelphia" and the city's undisputed boss. Vare had grown up on a pig farm in the Neck, as the rural stretches of South Philadelphia were once known. He and his two brothers had begun as garbage collectors before they moved into street cleaning and contracting. Eventually, they rose to manage millions of dollars in city contracts and to control the municipal government through savvy patronage and payoffs.

Mayor Kendrick was a loyal Vare ally. By moving the fair to South Philadelphia, Kendrick was delivering thousands of jobs to his patron's constituents, as well as improvements like sewers, paved roads and streetlighting. Vare also benefited personally, since the South Philadelphia land he owned skyrocketed in value. His contracting firm was paid handsomely to deliver nearly two million cubic yards of landfill from its excavations for the Broad Street Subway to prepare the swampy site for construction.

City architect John Molitor, assisted by a recent University of Pennsylvania graduate named Louis I. Kahn, drew up plans for a dazzling Rainbow City. The Sesqui buildings would be painted in bright pastels and illuminated by colored lights at night. The major pavilions were designed in a streamlined style that might have been inspired by the art deco fashion popularized in a 1925 Paris exposition. But the buildings' clean lines and lack of ornamentation also meant that they could be built cheaply and quickly.

From the moment visitors entered the Sesqui, they would be overwhelmed by the celebration of modern technology, which was the fair's primary mission.

An artist's conception of the Babelesque Tower of Light atop the Stairway of Nations, as it was supposed to look at Philadelphia's 1926 Sesqui-Centennial Exposition.

A gigantic replica of the Liberty Bell, rising eighty feet high and studded with twenty-six thousand light bulbs, would bridge South Broad Street just below Oregon Avenue. This electric marvel would be set in a park named Marconi Plaza, honoring the developer of another modern wonder, the radio.

Once visitors passed under the Liberty Bell, they would proceed south to the fair's main entrance at Packer Avenue. There, Broad Street would open into a monumental plaza called the Forum of the Founders, surrounded by the fair's five main palaces: Liberal Arts & Manufactures; Food & Agriculture; Education; Fine Arts; and Transportation, Machinery, Mines & Metallurgy.

Here, visitors would admire the second wonder of the Sesqui: the Tower of Light, highest point in the fair. Located between the Palaces of Liberal Arts & Manufactures and Food & Agriculture, this two-hundred-foot-tall phallus would stand atop the coronary-inducing Stairway of Nations. From its rounded dome, the Light of Independence—composed of the world's two largest searchlights—would turn night into day for miles around. Sesqui publicists promised that the Tower of Light would "appear when illuminated at night as a great silver shaft shedding its radiance over the entire Exposition grounds."

On the west side of the Forum of the Founders, the Gladway would feature amusements that would put the Ferris wheel at Chicago's 1893 Columbian

Exposition to shame. The biggest attraction would be a full-scale replica of King Solomon's Temple, which would rise hundreds of feet high in white and gold splendor. Every hour, clouds of gas would be released to simulate the destruction of the temple by the Babylonians.

Unfortunately, political and economic realities forced planners to scale back their artistic visions for the Rainbow City. President Calvin Coolidge did not give official recognition to the fair until April 1925. Congress, perhaps peeved over being excluded from the initial planning, waited until March 1926 to allocate $2.2 million in federal aid, including the cost of its own buildings. This amount was chicken feed for a world's fair, even in 1926.

The Pennsylvania State Government allocated $1 million for the construction of a state pavilion. Governor Gifford Pinchot, a foe of the Vare syndicate, made sure that not one penny of state funds went to support the fair itself. The rest of the Sesqui had to be underwritten by the city treasury and private donations. In 1925, a $3 million bond issue for the Sesqui was over-subscribed by private citizens, but that amount covered less than half of the fair's estimated cost.

The Coolidge administration also dragged its feet before inviting foreign nations and American states to the exposition. Sensing that this would not be a fair to remember, only nine states and six countries elected to construct pavilions at the Sesqui. Most of the participating nations were distinctly B-list: Argentina, Cuba, Czechoslovakia, Japan, Persia and Sweden. The merchants of India pledged to build a replica of the Taj Mahal, while ten other countries deigned to display smaller exhibits in the palaces.

Despite attempts to scale back, the Sesqui was broke before it began. The city had to pay over $2 million to drain and fill the League Island Park marshes before excavation could begin on one building. When contracting bids for the five palaces came in, they were hundreds of thousands of dollars over estimate. It soon became apparent that city architect John Molitor's budget of $7.1 million was at least $5 million too low. Director David C. Collier relieved the indignant Molitor of his duties. Soon after, Collier handed in his own resignation, disgusted by the unrealistic financial and scheduling constraints placed on him.

In January 1926, with opening day less than six months away, most of the Sesqui's one thousand acres looked like a Great War battlefield: muddy plains scarred by empty trenches and shells of buildings. Only the Palaces of Liberal Arts & Manufactures and Food & Agriculture were near completion, as was the municipal stadium in the fair's southeast corner. The other three palaces were all in the early stages of construction, as were most of the state and foreign pavilions. Plans for Solomon's Temple and other exhibits were scrapped. Federal officials begged Mayor Kendrick to postpone the fair for a year, as Chicago had done when the Columbian Exposition was moved from 1892 to 1893.

But Kendrick, who had taken to riding around the fairgrounds on a handsome white steed like a plantation overseer, refused. Instead, he moved up opening day from June 1 to May 31. Kendrick was imperial potentate of the Shriners of North America, one of the many fraternal organizations in which he held office. He had persuaded the Shriners to hold their national convention in Philadelphia by promising to open the Sesqui-Centennial on the same day as their conference and to dedicate the first three days of the world's fair to them. The Sesqui was going to open on May 31, 1926, Kendrick insisted, come hell or high water.

And it did. On May 31, thousands of Shriners from around the country attended the inauguration of the Sesqui. They helped to fill out a sparse crowd of roughly twenty thousand spectators, since threatening gray skies kept many visitors away. It had rained for days before the fair opened, hindering last-minute construction and providing a harbinger of things to come. At Marconi Plaza, slicker-clad visitors watched the inaugural parade pass beneath a giant Liberty Bell shrouded in scaffolding. Afterward, they had to slog through several inches of mud to reach the opening ceremonies at the Sesqui Stadium. In the eighty-thousand-seat arena, the *Bulletin* reported that there appeared to be ten ushers for each visitor, and that "the only congestion is caused by hot dog, sandwich, and pennant salesmen."

In 1876, the high-powered team of President Grant and Brazilian emperor Dom Pedro had opened the centennial. In 1926, the star attractions were Secretary of Commerce Herbert Hoover and Secretary of State Frank B. Kellogg, neither of whom was a scintillating speaker. Hoover lectured the dispirited crowd on the "national misfortune" of the "growing disrespect for the law." Kellogg was upstaged by a black dog that ran onto the field, chased by a number of bored policemen and Boy Scouts.

Pennsylvania governor Gifford Pinchot was absent, having been informed by Mayor Kendrick that there would be no time for him to speak. President Coolidge didn't even send a congratulatory telegram. The crowd saved its loudest applause for local boy William S. Vare, who had just been nominated as U.S. senator. (Vare would win the election in November, but the Senate would refuse to seat him on grounds of fraud and corruption.)

After the opening ceremonies, visitors fanned throughout the fairgrounds, still a sea of mud broken by islands of scaffolding. The only fully operational structure was the government's model post office. The two palaces open to visitors—Liberal Arts & Manufactures and Food & Agriculture—were half empty, with many exhibits still in transit or in crates. Between them stood the metal skeleton of the unfinished Tower of Light, looking like a forest watch tower without its searchlights and granite sheathing. Across the Forum, the Gladway was anything but glad, with most amusements weeks away from completion.

Signs of shoddy, last-minute construction were everywhere. Wet plaster dripped on visitors in the Pennsylvania State Pavilion. Throughout the fairgrounds, recently dumped landfill had not been compacted, causing structures to sink and tilt. At the Sesqui Stadium, cracks already snaked across the brick walls and concrete door frames. The elegant balustrades lining the Gladway Lagoon were crumbling before many Gladway attractions had opened.

The only moment of the opening day that captured the public's imagination occurred when the giant Liberty Bell was illuminated. At 9:30 p.m., Mayor Kendrick's limousine roared up to Marconi Plaza, its custom-made siren blaring at top volume. The mayor and his wife posed for photographers by the light switch. At exactly 10:05 p.m., Mrs. Kendrick flipped the switch. More than twenty-six thousand amber-, ivory- and rose-colored lights blazed into life, drawing a roar of approval from thousands of spectators. The dazzling spectacle was visible two miles north at City Hall, which had also been turned into an illuminated fairy palace with strings of red, blue and purple lights, along with eight hundred colored spotlights.

The next day, the local press searched for a silver lining. The *Bulletin* pointed out that the recent downpours made the bright colors of the newly painted buildings shine and had settled the choking dust of the barren grounds. Out-of-town papers were blunter. The *New York American* stated that the Sesqui had "opened before it was ready and made the additional mistake of promising more than it had." This opinion was echoed by many of Mayor Kendrick's twenty-five thousand fellow Shriners, who returned home and told their neighbors not to waste the train fare on "Kendrick's Karnival."

After stumbling out of the gate, the Sesqui recovered somewhat. By August 1, most exhibits were in place. Those who paid the fifty-cent admission saw magnificent things. The Sesqui was many Americans' introduction to talking motion pictures, electric typewriters, office dictating machines, electric refrigerators and public address systems. People who had never ventured beyond Manayunk or Kensington could visit the Taj Mahal, a Persian bazaar and a Japanese teahouse.

Unfinished on the outside, the Spanish Pavilion was a treasure chest inside, filled with masterpieces by Goya and Velasquez, tapestries from the Spanish royal palace and precious gems valued at more than $10 million. At the Palace of Fine Arts, over ten thousand works of art were on display, including paintings by Thomas Eakins, Marc Chagall, Vasili Kandinsky, Claude Monet and Camille Pissarro. Elsewhere, visitors could see the anchor of the *Santa Maria*, Thomas Jefferson's carriage and Benjamin Franklin's scientific equipment.

Despite its cracks, the new municipal stadium hosted a string of gargantuan spectacles. Audiences were dazzled by *America*, a historical pageant featuring 10,000 actors, a 5,000-member chorus, a 1,500-piece band and a 200-member orchestra. While *America* was a one-shot deal, a smaller pageant (only 1,500 actors) entitled *Freedom* ran throughout the summer. On July 5, President Calvin Coolidge addressed a huge crowd. But the stadium's red-letter day was September 23, when over 120,000 spectators watched Gene Tunney defeat Jack Dempsey for the world heavyweight title.

Despite these high points, the Sesqui never found its footing. Attendance rose steadily throughout the summer, from 271,000 in June to over 1.2 million in September. But with no organized publicity to counter the negative word-of-mouth, the number of visitors remained well below expectations.

The Sesqui's worst enemy was the incessant rain, which dampened 107 of the fair's 184 days. Storm clouds gathered every time the crowds did: on the fair's opening and closing days, on nineteen of its twenty-six weekends, on Independence Day and during the Dempsey-Tunney fight. Not only did the rain keep visitors away, but it also permeated the poorly built structures. While Coolidge was addressing crowds at Sesqui Stadium on July 5, workers were cutting holes in the roof of the Palace of Food & Agriculture to keep it from collapsing under the tons of water that had pooled there.

After September, attendance plummeted. Suggestions to continue the fair in 1927 were quickly shelved. Mayor Kendrick did convince the Sesqui managers to extend its closing date one month, from December 1, 1926, to January 1, 1927. But most exhibitors started packing on December 1, and demolition began on many smaller structures. Meanwhile, the Persian pavilion was finally completed. With no visitors to see them, the native attendants wrapped rugs from the bazaar around their bodies, trying to stay warm in Philadelphia's wintry chill.

The unfinished skeleton of the Tower of Light as it actually appeared, looming behind the Food & Agriculture Palace. *Courtesy Robert Morris Skaler.*

When the Sesqui took its last breath at midnight on January 1, 1927, it was a ghost town. On the Forum of the Founders, the once-colorful palaces and pylons stood tall and gaunt and silent. The metal skeleton of the still-unfinished Tower of Light overlooked the deserted landscape, the tiny searchlight tacked on top extinguished forever. No ceremonies marked the official closing. A single attendant locked the main gate and walked home in the rain.

But the real excitement of the Sesqui was just beginning, as its managers tallied the damages. Originally, the Sesqui-Centennial Exposition Association had expected between 25 and 30 million visitors. Instead, paid admissions totaled 4,622,211, less than half than had paid to see the Centennial fifty years before. Kendrick and the other managers attempted to put a brave face on the figures. Despite low attendance, they estimated that the Sesqui deficit would be $200,000, a painful but manageable sum.

And then the bills began to pour in, from all of the architects, designers, builders, suppliers, performers and exhibitors who had helped to create the Rainbow City. There were also bills and lawsuits from property owners who had leased their land to the Sesqui and were complaining of damages. Among the latter group was one William S. Vare.

The size of the Sesqui deficit spiraled upward to nearly $6 million. More than four hundred creditors were represented by George C. Klauder, law partner of Harry A. Mackey, who was also city treasurer ("conflict of interest" was a relatively foreign concept in 1920s Philadelphia). Unable to cope with the flood of red ink, the Sesqui-Centennial Exposition Association declared bankruptcy. The auction price for a $1,000 Sesqui bond, of the kind purchased by hundreds of average Philadelphians to support *their* world's fair, collapsed to $40.

Mayor Kendrick ordered the city government to uphold its promise to make good on all Sesqui debts. But City Controller Will B. Hadley, who had his eye on the mayor's office, claimed that many fair bills were fraudulent and a ruse to enrich Kendrick's political cronies. He went so far as to subpoena the mayor and to sue for release of the fair's financial records. But the untouchable Kendrick avoided any legal action. Instead, he did an end run around Hadley, persuading the state legislature to pass a bill authorizing the City Council to settle all Sesqui debts.

To help pay the bills, the city government held the Great Yard Sale of 1927, a massive auction of Sesqui structures and goods that ran through March and April. The auction took place on the desolate fairgrounds, where waist-high weeds surrounded the crumbling pavilions. In the frenzied, uncontrolled bidding, properties were sold for pennies on the dollar—sometimes pennies on the hundreds of dollars.

The Sesqui managers had spent $3 million to build the fair's five main palaces. Their combined auction proceeds were approximately $61,000, or 2 percent of their original cost. The twenty-thousand-seat auditorium had been designed as a permanent structure to serve South Philadelphia after the fair ended. Built at a cost of $500,000, it was sold for $11,000, dismantled and shipped to a Bronx amusement park. The auditorium organ—one of the largest in the world, purchased for $150,000—was almost sold to a curio dealer for $1,250. At the last moment, publisher Cyrus H.K. Curtis bought it for a much larger sum and donated it to the University of Pennsylvania.

The Pennsylvania State Building—considered the most architecturally significant structure at the fair—was sold for $9,274 and demolished for its steel. It had originally cost $490,000. The Taj Mahal, given to the City of Philadelphia by the merchants of India, was sold for $600. The Cuban, Japanese and Spanish pavilions, also donated by their host nations, each fetched less than $200.

The Sesqui's two landmarks—the Liberty Bell and the Tower of Light—suffered particularly ignoble fates. After the fair ended, both structures had become dormitories for local tramps. The giant bell, with its twenty-six thousand light bulbs, ninety-seven tons of steel and miles of copper wire, was sold for $60 and dismantled. The incomplete Tower of Light, nicknamed "the Light that Failed," fetched $1,050. The bare steel skeleton had cost the city $365,093 before it gave up on it.

All of the fair buildings were either demolished or moved, with five exceptions: Sesqui Stadium (renamed John F. Kennedy Stadium in 1964 and demolished in 1992), the John Morton Memorial (finished in 1927 and now the American Swedish Historical Museum), a model recreation center (today a Fairmount Park facility) and a concrete gazebo and boathouse (built when League Island Park was partially developed in 1914, recycled for the Sesqui and still standing beside Edgewater Lake). From the sale of over $10 million worth of Sesqui assets, the city realized roughly $375,000.

In 1936, a reporter visited the Sesqui site on the tenth anniversary of the world's fair. She found a bleak, desolate landscape in the shadow of the United States Naval Hospital. On the concrete floor of the former auditorium, Philadelphians ruined by the Depression lived in tar-paper shacks, surrounded by automobile graveyards.

In the final analysis, Philadelphia spent over $23 million on the fair and lost nearly $10 million. Kendrick was able to float a bond issue to cover the expenses. But the costs of the Sesqui—along with the parkway, Broad Street Subway, Free Library, Museum of Art and other major construction projects of the high-flying '20s—drove Philadelphia to near-bankruptcy once the Depression hit.

More importantly, the Sesqui—described by one wag as "the flop heard round the world"—left deep scars on the Philadelphia psyche long before the 1929 crash. In countless newspaper articles, editorials and letters, Philadelphians agonized over the reasons for the fair's failure. They blamed the rain, the location, the size, the architecture, the lack of support from Harrisburg and Washington and Prohibition. Surprisingly few people pointed the finger at local politicians.

Instead, they began to blame themselves. In October 1926, as the Sesqui crawled toward its close, Mrs. Edward Beecher Fink of the Philadelphia Speakers' Bureau complained bitterly to the *New York Times* that "the people of the City of Brotherly Love have been the most ardent 'knockers' of all." This statement was probably a shock to the thousands of Philadelphians who not only braved inclement weather and a long trolley ride to frequent the fair but also spent their hard-earned dollars to purchase now-worthless Sesqui bonds. But many of them took it to heart.

Sin in the City of Brotherly Love

Philadelphia, characterized by Lincoln Steffens as "corrupt and contented" in 1904, remained corrupt yet grew increasingly discontented after 1926. Philadelphians had been willing to tolerate a city government rife with graft and fraud as long as it offered them basic services, financial security and self-esteem. But in 1926, the short-sighted self-interest of local politicians not only cost the city a fortune but also made it the laughing stock of the nation. Always good for a snicker, the Quaker City became the punch line for countless vaudevillians' jokes after the fair. Thanks to the Sesqui debacle, Philadelphia's self-confidence was the true light that failed.

WHAT LIES BENEATH

The Lafayette Cemetery Scandal, 1946

Everyone's out for that almighty dollar
Now if only the dead could holler.
If the dead could holler, then the land would be
One continual howl of pain and indignity.
—Margaret Alice Butler, Bensalem Township resident

It started out as a routine construction project at Rosedale Memorial Park on Neshaminy Boulevard in Bensalem, Bucks County, two miles north of Philadelphia. In 1988, a twenty-three-acre parcel of empty land on the cemetery's northern edge was sold to developer Jeffrey Blank for the Neshaminy Square Shopping Center. To make room for Blank's development, the Rosedale office and chapel were to be moved from the site to another unused tract farther west, where workers were digging excavations for the facilities.

And then—like a surprise ending from that summer's drive-in favorite, *Poltergeist III*—bodies began to pop out of the ground.

On Friday, September 16, 1988, Bensalem Township officials paid a surprise visit to Rosedale Memorial Park. An anonymous tipster had warned them that workers excavating new foundations for the cemetery office and chapel had uncovered two bodies in the supposedly vacant site. Now they were trying to rebury the remains in an unmarked grave, secretly and illegally.

At Rosedale, officials discovered two smashed burial vaults and two coffins, one of which had been dented, scratched and opened. They immediately issued a cease and desist order on all excavation. Meanwhile, I. Alan Cohen, owner of Rosedale Memorial Park, professed ignorance of the graves and told officials that no records existed for them.

On Monday, September 19, a public works crew scoured the excavation site with metal detectors. By the end of the day, small flags marked at least five other locations on the site that might have contained unmarked graves. After spending a week and a half digging test shafts, officials estimated that the "empty" cemetery land contained at least thirty trenches, each three hundred feet long and twenty feet wide. The trenches were crammed with thousands of wooden boxes stacked atop one another, all containing human remains.

At the same time, two reporters for the *Bucks County Courier-Times*, Adam Bell and Tery Schneider, uncovered an unsavory explanation for the anonymous graves. Poring over court records and historical documents, the two journalists determined that Rosedale's unmarked trenches held the remains of forty-seven thousand former inhabitants of Lafayette Cemetery in South Philadelphia, victims of a backroom political swindle from the 1940s.

Founded in 1839, Lafayette Cemetery stood on the square bordered by Ninth, Tenth, Wharton and Federal Streets. The five-acre burial ground was one of several neighborhood cemeteries established throughout Philadelphia's outlying districts, serving Moyamensing Township before it became part of South Philadelphia in 1854. The well-kept graveyard sheltered the remains of many local notables, including Thomas "Reddy" Miller, who played for the Philadelphia Athletics baseball team in 1874 before joining the St. Louis Brown Stockings.

By the early twentieth century, the once-tidy cemetery had become an overcrowded eyesore, filled with trash and broken gravestones. Designed to hold fourteen thousand bodies, Lafayette was packed with over forty-seven thousand corpses when its last occupant—eighty-five-year-old Eliza Ritter—was laid to rest there in 1942. According to cemetery records, one single grave held nearly fifty bodies.

City leaders had discussed replacing the cemetery with a playground as early as the 1920s, but the Depression and World War II prevented them from taking any action. Finally, by 1946, the city was ready to remove the urban blemish that Lafayette Cemetery had become. Unfortunately, Lafayette would look like a fragrant spring garden compared to the public display of greed and corruption that was about to erupt.

Lafayette Cemetery in South Philadelphia, seen from the corner of Ninth Street and Passyunk Avenue, shortly before its removal in 1946. *Urban Archives, Temple University.*

In March 1946, the city contracted with Thomas A. Morris, president of Evergreen Memorial Park in Bensalem Township, Bucks County, to dig up the forty-seven thousand sets of remains from Lafayette. Morris would be responsible for transferring the remains to individual plots at Evergreen, providing new caskets or burial containers as needed, as well as bronze grave markers, roadways and perpetual maintenance. The forty-acre plot at Evergreen, also to be known as Lafayette Cemetery, would be marked by a statue of the French general. Morris agreed to establish a $10,500 maintenance fund for the new burial ground and to pay $7,172 in back wages to the old Lafayette caretaker.

In exchange for his estimated outlay of $105,000, Thomas Morris received clear title to the Lafayette Cemetery land, which was assessed at $166,000. Morris promptly transferred this title to the Jamestown Realty Company. Morris and his partners at Jamestown planned to offer the city the entire property for $200,000 for use as a playground. If the city balked at their high price, then they would build apartments along the

Ninth Street side of the square and sell the city the rest of the tract for $100,000. Morris and his fellow principals stood to make a handsome profit under either scenario. If the city bought the entire property, they would double their money; otherwise, they would cover their costs and earn a steady income on the rental properties.

Thomas Morris, whom one judge described as "the type of guy who could sell the Brooklyn Bridge," was vice-president of Jamestown Realty. The president of Jamestown Realty was the sheriff of Philadelphia, Austin Meehan. (As I've mentioned elsewhere, "conflict of interest" has little meaning to many Philadelphia politicians.) As Republican leader of the Thirty-fifth Ward in Northeast Philadelphia, Meehan controlled postwar Philadelphia with the same iron fist as William S. Vare in the 1920s. Described by *Time* magazine as "a triple-chinned 200-pounder who liked to gobble ice cream by the quart," Meehan was accused by his opponents of using gangster tactics to intimidate Philadelphians and to shake down local corporations and utilities.

At the end of 1946, Morris removed all forty-seven thousand sets of human remains from their resting places at Lafayette Cemetery. South Philadelphia residents told of watching workers put the skeletal remains in small wooden boxes, or even in burlap bags, before loading them on trucks. By early 1947, Lafayette's once-lumpy terrain was smooth and ready for development. A complex system was set up to coordinate the location of graves at Lafayette with the plots at Evergreen. After the move, Morris wrote, "We were conscious of our responsibility in this sacred work and trust to God that the loved ones are now in a final resting place where beauty and dignity will always predominate."

The city was so pleased with Morris's competent yet compassionate work that in 1947 it awarded him the contract to disinter eight thousand bodies from Franklin Cemetery at Elkhart and Helen Streets in the Kensington district. These remains were to be reburied at Evergreen Memorial Park as well, in their own section with individual markers.

Within a few months, one of Philadelphia's nastiest mayoral campaigns had transformed Lafayette and Franklin Cemeteries from sweetheart deals into political hot potatoes. Patrician Richardson Dilworth was running for mayor on the Democratic ticket in 1947, relentlessly exposing the widespread corruption of the entrenched Republican administration. Rather than attacking incumbent mayor Bernard Samuel, Dilworth went after Sheriff Austin Meehan (whom he called "the fat Sultan"), the power behind the throne. Dilworth accused Mcehan of using his inside

Lafayette Cemetery at Tenth and Wharton Streets in 1947, after its bodies had been removed to Evergreen Memorial Park in Bensalem. *Urban Archives, Temple University.*

knowledge of municipal zoning to have Morris purchase Lafayette cheaply and then resell it at an inflated price to the city, which had already tagged the graveyard as a future playground.

Despite Dilworth's charges, a city-appointed panel agreed to pay Jamestown Realty $153,350 for the entire Lafayette property—a return of only 50 percent rather than the 100 percent anticipated by Meehan and Morris. Lafayette was turned into a municipal playground, as was the former Franklin Cemetery.

Although Dilworth lost the 1947 election to Samuel, his barbed attacks on Meehan and the Republican machine had an impact. In 1951, Dilworth's colleague Joseph S. Clark won the mayoralty, ending the Republicans' seventy-three-year stranglehold on Philadelphia politics. Dilworth served as district attorney during the Clark administration and then succeeded Clark as mayor from 1956 until 1962.

As Meehan and his fellow Republicans lost control of City Hall, Thomas Morris was losing his grip on his empire of death. In 1951, the Securities and Exchange Commission (SEC) investigated Morris for selling blocks of

Evergreen Memorial Park burial lots to speculators, promising that they could resell them for huge profits. This constituted a securities sale in the SEC's eyes, and Morris was not registered to sell securities. After being charged with fraud, Morris declared bankruptcy and sold his cemetery in 1959. Evergreen was subdivided into two separate memorial parks: the nonsectarian Rosedale and the Jewish King David. Morris died in 1976 at age eighty-two and was buried at King David.

During this upheaval, people forgot about the human remains removed from Lafayette and Franklin Cemeteries in 1946 and 1947. With few descendants present to make inquiries, it was assumed that they had been reburied at Evergreen under the conditions set by the court of common pleas, and the matter soon faded from the public consciousness.

The discovery of the trenches at Rosedale Memorial Park in 1988 shed some light on the fate of those buried at Lafayette and Franklin. Morris, perhaps stung that his investment had not yielded the rewards he had anticipated, tried to cut corners. He dug vast trenches in the northernmost part of Evergreen, filled them with the wooden boxes from Lafayette and covered them without a trace. According to township officials, some remains were dumped along isolated stretches of the Poquessing Creek in Bensalem. None of the niceties Morris had agreed to in his city contract—coffins, individual markers, roadways, a statue of Lafayette or a perpetual care trust—were ever honored. After Evergreen was sold and subdivided, the owners of the new Rosedale Memorial Park even opened a pet cemetery over some of the Lafayette graves.

One mystery that remained unsolved was what happened to the eight thousand sets of remains removed from Franklin Cemetery in Kensington. Some may lie in the Lafayette trenches. One court document suggests that three thousand Franklin bodies were buried near Galloway and Richlieu Roads, in what was then the southeast corner of Evergreen Memorial Park. But without official documentation, there is no way of knowing for sure. Today, at least five thousand bodies from Franklin Cemetery remain missing.

As the body count mounted throughout the autumn of 1988, Bensalem Township officials appeared stunned. They were suburban bureaucrats whose expertise ran to school bond issues, not what to do with fifty thousand unexpected corpses. I. Alan Cohen, owner of Rosedale Memorial Park, continued to insist that he had no records of the 1946 Lafayette removal, although state law would have required the previous owners to receive such documentation.

Jeffrey Blank, developer of the shopping center that was to be built adjacent to the mass grave, didn't understand why the nearby presence of human remains should delay his construction. Blank explained that when he bought his twenty-three-acre parcel from the Cohens in 1986, they had assured him that there were no bodies there, and that was good enough for him. "The funny thing," he told one reporter, "is that they found bones in a cemetery and people are making a fuss over it."

In November 1988, Bensalem Township and Rosedale Memorial Park reached an agreement under which the cemetery would find a new site for its office and chapel and preserve the mass graves as a permanent memorial. The Cohen family also agreed to erect a monument to the Lafayette Cemetery removals.

Meanwhile, the earth continued to give up its dead, this time on the site of the nearly completed Neshaminy Square Shopping Center. In December 1989, utility workers uncovered a burial vault on the shopping center property, four feet from the border with Rosedale. One township official suggested that the discovery was not an isolated case, saying that two excavators working on Neshaminy Square had told him, "We've been finding bones in this site since we started digging here."

After much negotiation between the lawyers for Rosedale Memorial Park, Jeffrey Blank and Bensalem Township, an agreement was reached that returned the land where the burial vault was found to Rosedale. In exchange for ceding the property, Blank received temporary occupancy permits for his shopping center, allowing him to open on schedule in early 1990. Bensalem Township also agreed, at least tacitly, to ignore reports of other human remains being discovered on the shopping center site.

In April 1990, the Cohen family finally erected a memorial to the anonymous bodies buried in trenches on their property. The small granite stone bears a bronze plaque with the grammatically incorrect inscription, "On this site lies the remains of those buried in Lafayette Cemetery Phila., PA. May they rest in peace." Since then, historical societies have installed plaques honoring such individuals as Civil War Congressional Medal of Honor winners Matthew McClelland and Edward B. Young, whose remains lie somewhere in the thirty trenches at Rosedale.

Despite the Cohens' token acknowledgment, an official amnesia still persists about the removals from Lafayette and Franklin Cemeteries. A recent visitor to Rosedale Memorial Park who asked about the mass graves blogged:

The only memorial to the forty-seven thousand men, women and children who once rested at Lafayette Cemetery, erected over their unmarked graves at Rosedale in 1990.

The office staff knows nothing about it. They know that two cemeteries closed and that the Lafayette bodies were buried at one end of Rosedale Memorial Park, while the other cemetery's bodies were interred at the other end…but not which end was which. Nor who was moved. Nor what happened to their stones. Nor even if there was a monument, a plaque, etc., to the mass grave.

May they rest in peace.

GOOD NIGHT, SWEET PRINCE

John Barrymore Comes Home, 1980

Die? I should say not, my dear fellow. No Barrymore would ever allow such a conventional thing to happen to him.
—John Barrymore, apocryphal last words

You heard me, Mike.
—John Barrymore, actual last words

The two policemen crept up behind the tall, thin man as he banged on the oak doors of the mansion, surrounded by a copse of trees and set far back from the highway. It was a cold December night in 1980. The police had received a nervous call a few minutes earlier from the archbishop's residence, home of the top prelate of the Catholic Church in Philadelphia. An unidentified intruder had gotten onto the large, wooded estate at 5700 City Avenue in the residential Wynnefield section. Now, the two officers responding to the call watched the stranger batter the massive doors of the palatial residence with his fists while he yelled for the archbishop to come out.

The officers positioned themselves behind the frantic man and glanced at each other. One removed his gun from his holster. The intruder looked unarmed, but they didn't want to take any chances. Crime had been on the rise in Philadelphia, especially after the assassination of Mafia boss Angelo Bruno in April had triggered a gang war. Drug use was increasing, too, and reports had surfaced of a highly addictive version of cocaine called crack, which made its users extremely paranoid and violent. Three police officers had been shot to death so far in 1980, the most in five years.

As the officer released the safety on his gun, his partner turned his flashlight on the stranger, silhouetting him against the entrance.

"Sir! Will you please turn around and step away from the door!"

Oblivious, the man continued to pound away. The first officer raised his gun.

"Sir!" the second officer shouted. "Please step away from the door and raise your hands NOW!"

The intruder spun around, recoiling from the flashlight's beam like a vampire. As he slowly raised his arms, the officers checked him out. In his forties, maybe fifties. Dressed in jeans, jacket and open-necked shirt, despite the frigid winter night. Shaggy hair and a beard obscured a haggard yet handsome face, with high cheekbones and a prominent nose. Even in the flashlight's glare, the pupils of the man's deep-set eyes were dilated. Definitely high on something.

"Oh. Hello." The man's voice was gentle and confused. "Can you guys help me out?" He started to approach them but stopped when he was ordered to freeze. He stood passively, swaying slightly, as the officer with the flashlight patted him down. No weapons. He surrendered his wallet without protest. The first officer stared at the ID and then showed it to his partner.

A California driver's license. John Drew Barrymore. Born June 4, 1932.

"What are you doing here, Mr. Barrymore?"

"I really need to talk to the archbishop."

The officer with the flashlight smelled the faint aroma of grass. He relaxed a little. This guy was stoned. Not likely to attack them, despite his assault on the doors.

"Why do you need to see the archbishop, Mr. Barrymore?"

"For my dad. The archbishop needs to bless my dad."

"Where is your father, Mr. Barrymore?"

Barrymore glanced around nervously. "Oh, there he is." Relieved, he pointed at a suitcase on the porch of the mansion.

"Okay." The officer felt his muscles tense again. "Mr. Barrymore, we'd like you to come with us. No, you stay here. I'll get your father."

Over numerous cups of coffee at the Nineteenth District Station, the meaning of the midnight visit gradually emerged. First, John Drew Barrymore had smoked some really dynamite weed on his flight from Los Angeles to Philadelphia, a fact he repeatedly shared with the entire station. Second, his father—or rather, a can containing his father's cremated

John Barrymore, "the Great Profile," as he appeared when his Hamlet was the toast of Broadway in 1922.

remains—was indeed in his suitcase. Finally, John Barrymore—the Philadelphia-born actor who dazzled both Broadway and Hollywood in the early twentieth century—had finally come home to rest.

John Sidney Blyth Barrymore was the brightest star in a theatrical dynasty that had already lasted three generations when he made his debut on February 15, 1882. He was born at 2008 Columbia (now Cecil B. Moore) Avenue in North Philadelphia, in the home of his grandmother, Louisa Lane (Mrs. John) Drew. Louisa had made her own stage debut in England at the age of five in 1825. Two years later, her actor parents immigrated to the United States. Louisa grew up to become one of the darlings of America's two great theatrical capitals, Philadelphia and New York. She played opposite all of the great actors of the day, including Edwin Forrest, Junius Brutus Booth and Joseph Jefferson.

In 1850, Louisa married actor John Drew, with whom she had three children: Louisa, John Jr. and Georgianna. In 1861, the Drews acquired the down-at-heels Arch Street Theatre at 609–615 Arch Street, planning to restore it and become actor-managers. The next year, John Drew died at the age of thirty-four, after falling down the stairs at a party for six-year-old Georgianna. The indomitable Louisa ran the theatre herself and restored it to its former glory by persuading her famous friends to act there. At the same time, she raised her three children alone and even adopted a fourth child, Sidney (although rumors persisted that he was her illegitimate son).

Two of Louisa's children—John Jr. and Georgianna ("Georgie") became well-known actors themselves. In 1876, Georgie married Maurice Barrymore, an actor friend of her brother John. Georgie and Maurice had three children, all born in Philadelphia: Lionel (1878), Ethel (1879) and John (1882). As Philadelphia's theatrical fortunes waned, the Barrymores spent much of their time in New York or touring on the road. Louisa became a surrogate parent to her grandchildren, who called her "Mum Mum."

Shortly after John was born, Louisa moved from Columbia Avenue to 140 North Twelfth Street, a short walk from her theatre. The three-story house (demolished when the Convention Center was built) had large, high-ceilinged rooms; a nursery known as "the Annex"; and an attic where John and Lionel slept. Lionel, four years older than John, kept cages of white mice in the attic. They got loose and infested the entire house, bringing the cook to the verge of a breakdown. On special occasions, the three children were taken to the gold-and-red-velvet paradise known as the Arch Street Theatre, where they would sit in their grandmother's private box to watch shows.

Besides the Barrymore children, 140 North Twelfth Street was home to Louisa's elderly mother, Eliza, and her two sons, John Jr. (Uncle Jack) and Sidney (Uncle Googan). Grandmother Eliza, who lived in the attic next to Lionel and John, had them recite a nightly prayer: "God bless Mother, and Papa, and Mum Mum, and Grandmother, and Uncle Googan, and please, God, make Uncle Jack a good actor." John Drew Jr. had a slow start in the theatre due to his sloppy diction, and he sold clocks at Wanamaker's to make ends meet. He later became a popular matinee idol.

Uncle Googan was a talented actor but preferred to spend his time hustling pool in the nearby Tenderloin. Young Lionel and John would accompany him to the billiard halls as his mascots, their cherubic faces helping to lull unsuspecting pigeons into games with the expert Sidney. The two boys also acted as advance guards, keeping an eye out for sore losers lying in wait for Uncle Googan.

All three children attended private schools in Philadelphia. Ethel went to Notre Dame Academy, an exclusive Catholic girls' school on Rittenhouse Square. As a small child, John attended a junior school at Notre Dame, where he enjoyed drawing pictures of devils and demons on the blackboard to scare the younger pupils. Lionel attended the old Episcopal Academy at Locust and Juniper Streets. But when he showed off his prep school education by calling the family maid a "sonofabitch," he was quickly transferred to a Catholic school. (The children's mother had converted from the Episcopal faith to Catholicism under the influence of actress Helena Modjeska.)

In 1889, Georgie and Maurice Barrymore settled in New York, which had eclipsed Philadelphia as America's theatrical crossroads. They brought with them eleven-year-old Lionel, ten-year-old Ethel and seven-year-old John. Three years later, Louisa Drew sold the Arch Street Theatre and moved to New York to join her family.

But the Barrymore clan began to splinter shortly after. In 1892, Georgie died of tuberculosis at a California sanitarium, with Ethel by her side. Maurice was on the road, and fourteen-year-old Ethel had to accompany her mother's body back East. Less than a year after Georgie's death, the notoriously unfaithful Maurice married another actress named Mamie Floyd, earning Louisa's enmity. Mamie later seduced her stepson John when he was only fourteen, not long before Maurice was committed to the Bellevue Hospital insane ward with dementia induced by alcoholism and syphilis. Lionel and Ethel, who had both made their acting debuts as children at Louisa's Arch Street Theatre, were soon on the road themselves, having begun their theatrical apprenticeships with various touring companies.

A special bond had always existed between Louisa and John, her youngest grandchild. With the rest of his family away, the motherless boy grew even closer to his Mum Mum. In 1897, fifteen-year-old John spent a happy summer with seventy-seven-year-old Louisa at a resort hotel in Larchmont, New York. They sat on the beach looking out on Long Island Sound; Louisa read while John, a talented amateur artist, sketched. They both knew she was terminally ill. "I saw you come into this world," she told him at one point, "and now you are seeing me out of it. A fair exchange." Louisa died of congenital heart failure at the end of the summer.

With her strict discipline and all-encompassing love, Louisa had been an anchor of strength for her quicksilver grandson. Until his death, John would remember her Philadelphia household as a sanctuary. When his own life grew increasingly chaotic, John longed increasingly for the warmth and stability of his grandmother's home. On theatrical opening nights, the Drew and Barrymore families always sent each other red apples as gifts. Speaking of Louisa years after her death, John said, "If such a thing be possible, I know that at Heaven's Gate Mum Mum was given, not a red apple, but one of purest gold when she entered there."

After flirting with a career as an artist, John decided to follow his parents and siblings into the theatre. His first professional appearance was in the Philadelphia tryout of Clyde Fitch's *Captain Jinks of the Horse Marines*, a star vehicle for his sister Ethel. When the show debuted at the Walnut Street Theatre in January 1901, John went on as a last-minute substitute for another actor. He muffed his few lines and then ad-libbed, "Where do we go from here?" At this point, Ethel went into a hysterical state that, John recalled later, "was a cross between hilarity and strangulation." John capped the evening by taking a solitary curtain call. He was dropped from the cast when the play moved to Broadway, where it made Ethel a star.

Despite this inauspicious debut, John soon joined Ethel and Lionel on Broadway, where the three became known as "the Royal Family of the American Theatre." He starred in numerous popular and classical plays and was acclaimed as the finest Hamlet of his generation. Around 1914, Barrymore began a film career that would enthrone him in Hollywood, as well as on Broadway. Between 1914 and 1941, he appeared in over fifty films, starring in such classics as *Don Juan, Dinner at Eight* and *Grand Hotel.* As a young man, his athletic physique made him one of Hollywood's first male sex symbols, while his striking features—especially his long, perfectly shaped nose—earned him the soubriquet "the Great Profile."

Sadly, John's love of liquor—which had first manifested itself in childhood, when he chugged the dregs of adults' cocktails at family parties—blossomed into full-blown alcoholism before he reached middle age. In 1920, while appearing on Broadway as Richard III, he suffered his first alcohol-induced nervous breakdown, publicly attributed to fatigue and overwork. Barrymore biographer Gene Fowler estimated that the actor consumed 640 barrels of hard liquor over forty years.

By the late 1930s, Barrymore could not remember lines and was reduced to supporting roles in B films like *The Invisible Woman.* He divorced his third wife, Dolores Costello, in 1935 to move in with and then marry a nineteen-year-old college student named Elaine Barrie. Elaine, Barrymore's fourth and final wife, was a would-be actress whose greatest cinematic achievement was a short subject entitled *How to Undress in Front of Your Husband.* The two divorced in 1937, reunited and divorced again in 1940.

On May 19, 1942, John Barrymore collapsed during rehearsals for Rudy Vallee's radio show, where he had a recurring role as a washed-up ham actor. He was taken to the Hollywood Presbyterian Hospital, floating in and out of unconsciousness for ten days while his family and friends stood by helplessly. The sixty-year-old actor died on May 29 of myocarditis, complicated by cirrhosis of the liver, chronic nephritis and gastric ulcers—all results of his alcoholism. His last words were "You heard me, Mike"—a response when his brother Lionel (whom John called Mike) asked John to repeat himself.

According to Hollywood legend, a group of Barrymore's hard-drinking cronies held a wake at the Cock and Bull Bar after his death. Among them were Errol Flynn, swashbuckling star of epics like *Robin Hood* and *Captain Blood,* and Raoul Walsh, one-eyed director of *The Roaring Twenties* and *High*

The Drew-Barrymore plot at Mount Vernon Cemetery, with the monument of John Barrymore's "Mum Mum," Louisa Lane Drew, in the rear. *Courtesy of Michael Brooks.*

Sierra. Flynn, one of the last to leave the bar that night, stumbled home to Beverly Hills and flicked on the hall lights. He stared into the bloated, white, bloodless face of the corpse of John Barrymore.

Screaming hysterically, Flynn ran outside, only to be stopped by Raoul Walsh and two other drinking buddies. After leaving the Cock and Bull, the three men had stopped by Pierce Brothers Mortuary on Sunset Boulevard and paid the night attendant $200 to "borrow" Barrymore's body. They drove to Flynn's house in Beverly Hills and propped the unembalmed corpse in a chair as a joke. After they calmed Flynn down, the three men returned Barrymore's remains to the morgue, while Flynn staggered upstairs to spend a sleepless night.

In his will, John Barrymore had expressed his desire to be cremated and to have his ashes buried in the Barrymore-Drew lot in Philadelphia's Mount Vernon Cemetery, next to his parents and beloved grandmother. Ethel and Lionel Barrymore overrode their brother's wishes. Instead, they had John's body entombed in the mausoleum at Calvary Cemetery, a Catholic burial ground in Los Angeles. They would later join John there, as would ex-wife Dolores Costello.

John Barrymore's remains rested at Calvary for nearly forty years until his only son decided to fulfill his father's wishes. John Drew Barrymore was born John Sidney Blyth Barrymore Jr. in 1932, the child of Barrymore and third wife Dolores Costello. An infant when his parents divorced in 1935, John Jr. remembered seeing his famous father only once. Despite his mother's objections, John decided to become an actor, just like his father.

Unfortunately, John had major substance abuse issues, just like his father. His acting career was curtailed by his drunkenness, drug use, violent outbursts and frequent incarcerations. His three marriages produced two children: John Sidney Blyth Barrymore III, born 1954, and Drew Barrymore (yes, *that* Drew Barrymore), born 1975. After John's death in 2004 at the age of seventy-two, one of his obituaries read that "he was best known for having embraced the Barrymore predilection for hard living and reckless drinking."

In December 1980, the reclusive Barrymore impulsively decided to have his father cremated and reburied in Philadelphia, supposedly after hearing a rendition of the Robert Service poem, "The Cremation of Sam McGee." He and his son had the body removed from Calvary and taken to the crematorium at Odd Fellows Cemetery. According to legend, John decided to look at his father's corpse once it was removed from its silver-plated copper coffin. He stumbled into the car afterward, white as a sheet, and told his son, "Thank God I'm drunk, I'll never remember it." Evidently, moving the coffin had dislodged the jaw from the rest of the skull. Although most of the flesh on the face had decomposed, the Great Profile's long nose cartilage remained intact.

A lawyer for the family called the Pennsylvania Burial Company in South Philadelphia to let it know that John Drew Barrymore would be coming East with his father's ashes. Two weeks later, with the help of some chemical courage, Barrymore flew to Philadelphia with his father's ashes on his lap. Arriving late at night, the confused Barrymore made his way to the city's western edge, fueled by the desire to have his father's ashes blessed before they were interred.

On December 12, 1980, the remains of John Barrymore were laid to rest at Mount Vernon Cemetery. In the presence of a single undertaker, John Drew Barrymore placed his father's ashes in the ground next to the grave of Louisa Lane Drew. "Now it is finished," John said. He then flew back to California. He left behind an unpaid bill to the Pennsylvania Burial Company for $930, which included a $200 cash advance, and no plans to commemorate or care for his father's grave. John Barrymore's resting place would remain unmarked for eighteen years, until a group of local fans raised funds to purchase a monument.

Today, Mount Vernon Cemetery, at Ridge and Allegheny Avenues, is a derelict and forlorn place. Its gates are usually locked, and visitors rarely stroll along its paths. Periodically, suggestions are made to move the Barrymore-Drew plot across Ridge Avenue to more upscale Laurel Hill

John Barrymore's grave at Mount Vernon Cemetery, where his ashes have rested since 1980. *Courtesy of John Schimpf.*

Cemetery. Others have suggested that America's foremost acting dynasty be taken across the Schuylkill River to West Laurel Hill Cemetery in Lower Merion, where they could join other retired actors in the burial lot for the Edwin Forrest Home.

Until that day arrives, one of the world's greatest actors remains hidden away at Mount Vernon Cemetery. John Barrymore's grave is marked only by a small granite oblong that reads, "Alas, Poor Yorick"—a reference to the finest Hamlet Broadway has ever seen.

SELECT BIBLIOGRAPHY

Baltzell, E. Digby. *Philadelphia Gentlemen: The Making of a National Upper Class.* Chicago: Quadrangle Paperbacks, 1971.

Burt, Nathaniel. *The Perennial Philadelphians: The Anatomy of an American Aristocracy.* Boston: Little, Brown & Co., 1963.

Cotter, John L., et al. *The Buried Past: The Architectural History of Philadelphia.* Philadelphia: University of Pennsylvania Press, 1992.

Crane, Elaine Forman, ed. *The Diary of Elizabeth Drinker.* Boston: Northeastern University Press, 1991.

Davis, Allen F., and Mark H. Haller. *The Peoples of Philadelphia: A History of Ethnic Groups and Lower-Class Life, 1790–1940.* Philadelphia: Temple University Press, 1973.

Fowler, Gene. *Good Night, Sweet Prince: The Life and Times of John Barrymore.* New York: The Viking Press, 1944.

Godbeer, Richard. *Sexual Revolution in Early America.* Baltimore: Johns Hopkins University Press, 2002.

Gross, Kali N. *Colored Amazons: Crime, Violence, and Black Women in the City of Brotherly Love, 1880–1910.* Durham, NC: Duke University Press, 2006.

Harper, Steven Craig. *Promised Land: Penn's Holy Experiment, the Walking Purchase, and the Dispossession of the Delawares, 1600–1763.* Bethlehem, PA: Lehigh University Press, 2006.

Jackson, John W. *With the British Army in Philadelphia 1777–1778.* San Rafael, CA: Presidio Press, 1979.

Johnson, David R. *Policing the Urban Underworld: The Impact of Crime on the Development of the American Police, 1800–1887.* Philadelphia: Temple University Press, 1979.

Kelley, Joseph J., Jr. *Life and Times in Colonial Philadelphia.* Harrisburg, PA: Stackpole Books, 1973.

King, Moses. *Philadelphia and Notable Philadelphians.* New York: Moses King Publisher, 1901.

Lane, Roger. *Violent Death in the City: Suicide, Accident and Murder in 19th Century Philadelphia.* Cambridge, MA: Harvard University Press, 1979.

———. *William Dorsey's Philadelphia and Ours: On the Past and Future of the Black City in America.* New York: Oxford University Press, 1991.

Lewis, Arthur H. *The Worlds of Chippy Patterson.* New York: Harcourt, Brace & Co., 1960.

Lippard, George. *The Quaker City, or, the Monks of Monk Hall.* Amherst: University of Massachusetts Press, 1995.

Lyons, Clare A. *Sex Among the Rabble: An Intimate History of Gender & Power in the Age of Revolution, Philadelphia, 1730–1830.* Chapel Hill: University of North Carolina Press, 2006.

McCaffery, Peter. *When Bosses Ruled Philadelphia: The Emergence of the Republican Machine, 1867–1933.* University Park: Pennsylvania State University Press, 1993.

Nash, Gary B. *First City: Philadelphia and the Forging of Historical Memory.* Philadelphia: University of Pennsylvania Press, 2002.

Newman, Simon P. *Embodied History: The Lives of the Poor in Early Philadelphia.* Philadelphia: University of Pennsylvania Press, 2003.

Reynolds, David S. *George Lippard.* Boston: Twayne Publishers, 1982.

Sappol, Michael. *A Traffic of Dead Bodies: Anatomy and Embodied Social Identity in Nineteenth-Century America.* Princeton, NJ: Princeton University Press, 2002.

Scharf, J. Thomas, and Thompson Westcott. *History of Philadelphia 1609–1884.* Philadelphia: L.H. Everts & Co., 1884.

Shultz, Suzanne M. *Body Snatching: The Robbing of Graves for the Education of Physicians in Early Nineteenth Century America.* Jefferson, NC: McFarland & Co., 2005.

Thompson, Ray. *The Walking Purchase Hoax of 1737.* Fort Washington, PA: Bicentennial Press, 1973.

Warner, Paul T. *History of the First Moravian Church of Philadelphia.* Nazareth, PA: Moravian Historical Society, 1944.

Warner, Sam Bass. *The Private City: Philadelphia in Three Periods of Its Growth.* Philadelphia: University of Pennsylvania Press, 1991.

Watson, John F. *Annals of Philadelphia, and Pennsylvania, in the Olden Time.* Philadelphia: J.M. Stoddart & Co., 1877.

Weigley, Russell F., et al. *Philadelphia: A 300-Year History.* New York: W.W. Norton & Company, 1982.

Westcott, Thompson. *The Historic Mansions and Buildings of Philadelphia, with Some Notice of Their Owners and Occupants.* Philadelphia: Porter & Coates, 1877.

Wolf, Edwin. *Philadelphia: Portrait of an American City.* Harrisburg, PA: Stackpole Books, 1975.

ABOUT THE AUTHOR

Thomas H. Keels is an *ausländer*—sociologist E. Digby Baltzell's term for an outsider who moves to Philadelphia and falls in love with its rich heritage.

Since moving to Philadelphia in 1988, Tom has written five books dealing with local history: *Wicked Philadelphia*; *Forgotten Philadelphia: Lost Architecture of the Quaker City*; *Philadelphia Graveyards and Cemeteries*; *Philadelphia's Rittenhouse Square* (with Robert Morris Skaler); and *Chestnut Hill* (with Liz Jarvis). His next book, *Rainbow Cities: Philadelphia's Three World's Fairs*, will be published in 2012.

Tom is a regular contributor to the *Rittenhouse Sq. Revue* and also contributes features to *Creatively Speaking* on WRTI-FM. A self-proclaimed taphophile, he has been a tour guide at Laurel Hill, Philadelphia's premier Victorian cemetery, for over a decade.

Visit us at
www.historypress.net